FACTS AT YOUR FINGERTIPS

INVENTION AND TECHNOLOGY

LAND AND WATER TRANSPORTATION

BROWN
BEAR
BOOKS

Published by Brown Bear Books Ltd

4877 N. Circulo Bujia
Tucson, AZ 85718
USA

and

First Floor
9-17 St. Albans Place
London N1 0NX

© 2012 Brown Bear Books Ltd

Library of Congress Cataloging-in-Publication Data

Jackson, Tom, 1972-
  Land and water transportation.
       p. cm. – (Facts at your fingertips.
              invention and technology)
  Includes index.
  ISBN 978-1-936333-42-4 (library binding)
1.   Transportation–Juvenile literature. 2.   Motor vehicles–Juvenile
literature. 3.   Boats and boating–Juvenile literature. I. Title.

  TA1149.J33 2013
  629.04–dc23
                                       2011046989

Editorial Director: Lindsey Lowe
Editor: Tom Jackson
Creative Director: Jeni Child
Designer: Lynne Lennon
Children's Publisher: Anne O'Daly
Production Director: Alastair Gourlay

Printed in the United States of America

Picture Credits

Front Cover: Shutterstock
Back Cover: Istock: Comstock

Alamy: CountrySideCollection/Homer Sykes 13; Norbert
Michalke/Imagbroker 20b; Qapphotos 31; **Shutterstock**: 30-31,
334t, 42tl; Kharidehal Abhirama Ashwin 6br; Can Balcioglu 18b;
John Blanton 39; Digital Sport Agency 44tl; Kathy Gold 17bl;
Igor Golovniov 36br, Margo Harrison 8t; Mirek Hejnicki 22b;
Wojtek Jarco 16br, Jorgedasi 10b; James Kingman 42cl; Jan
Kranendonk 29t; Marek Lambert 42br; R. J Lerich 29b; Dmitry
Nikolaev 12 inset; Mark William Penny 4; esting 44r; Stanislaw
Tokarski 41t; **Siemens**: 33; **Thinkstock**: Comstock 1, 15b, 18t,
22t, 27b; Digital Vision 3, 14t, 40; Goodshoot 7; Hemera 4 inset,
6bl, 8b, 15t, 21tr, 23br, 30b; istockphoto 6t, 9, 10t, 11, 19t, 20t,
21bl, 26t, 28, 36l, 38b, 41b, 45; Liquidlibrary 21br; Photodisc 12;
Photos.com 14cr, 16tl, 17tr, 24, 24-25, 25, 27t, 38t; **Topfoto**:
23bl, HIP 37; The Granger Collection 34b, 35

*Brown Bear Books has made every attempt to contact the
copyright holder. If you have any information please email
smortimer@windmillbooks.co.uk*

All artwork copyright Brown Bear Books Ltd

CONTENTS

ANIMAL POWER

Since the dawn of civilization humans have harnessed the strength of large animals to help them get around. Horses and other "beasts of burden" are used even today to transport people through rugged landscapes.

No one knows when people began to use tame animals to carry things. Perhaps it was around 6000 B.C., when the first cities were being built. It may have been in the settlements that grew up on the fertile plains of the Middle East, where the terrain is well-suited to animal transport. Oxen were probably the first animals to be used, then donkeys. We know oxen were dragging wooden sleds in Mesopotamia (part of modern Iraq) before 3500 B.C.

▼ *Animal-powered vehicles are not in common use today in most parts of the world. However, they are sometimes used for leisure activities such as carriage racing.*

SOCIETY AND INVENTIONS

Lands Without the Wheel

The wheel was probably invented several times over in different parts of the world. However, the ancient civilizations of the Americas, such as the Maya, Aztecs, and Incas, never used wheels. The likely reason for this is that wheeled wagons need strong draft animals such as oxen, good roads, and flat land. American animals, such as the llama (below), are too small to haul large carts. Instead these animals carry loads through mountains that are too rugged for wheeled vehicles to cross. In snowbound countries, too, wheels were useless: in Scandinavia, reindeer were used to pull sleds in winter. Even in the Middle East, where the wheel was invented, camels were used to make journeys across the roadless deserts.

A rope through a nose ring is all that is needed to lead a tame ox. Oxen can be harnessed simply: a pair can be placed on each side of a single shaft, with a wooden crosspiece resting as a yoke across their shoulders. In North Africa donkeys are still ridden without any bridle. To guide them, the rider touches them lightly between the ears with a stick.

The wheel

Oxen helped people move heavy loads. But they couldn't move fast, and the load was limited to what could be dragged along rough tracks. After 4000 B.C. tree trunks began to be used as rollers, making loads easier to pull. At around 3500 B.C., in Mesopotamia, wheels were added to sleds to make the first carts.

KEY COMPONENTS

Inventing the wheel

Before wheels were invented, loads were moved on sleds that ran over log rollers. A sled rolling across a log many times will cut a groove, and this might be how the first wheels and axles were invented. The narrow groove became the axle, while the wide roller formed the wheel. The axle was then attached to the sled, forming a simple cart. Later carts had fixed axles in which only the wheels could turn.

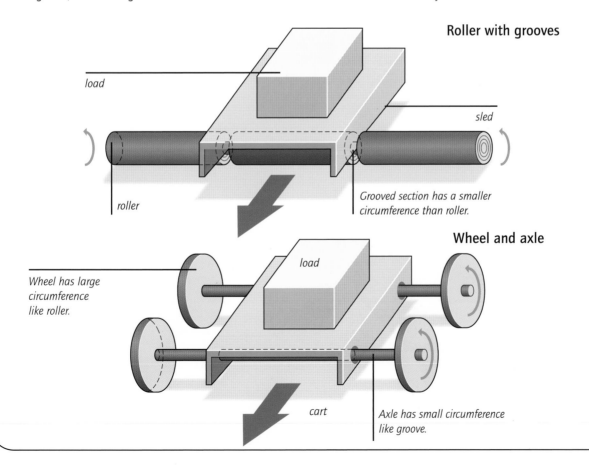

Roller with grooves

load

sled

roller

Grooved section has a smaller circumference than roller.

Wheel and axle

Wheel has large circumference like roller.

load

cart

Axle has small circumference like groove.

The first wheels were solid wooden disks, either cut from a single plank or made from two or three narrower planks fastened together with cleats (wedges of wood or metal).

The coming of the horse

Almost as important as the wheel was the discovery of how to domesticate horses—and ride them. Riding probably began about 5,000

▼ *The takhi, or Przewalski's horse, is a wild horse from Mongolia. It is very rare today but is probably very similar to the ancient horses that were first tamed by humans.*

large chest with big lungs

powerful leg muscles

long legs for running

▲ *Horses evolved for life on the wide open grasslands, such as here in Mongolia. The first domestic horses were probably tamed in this Central Asian region.*

WAR CHARIOTS

Wheeled vehicles were also soon used in warfare. In Mesopotamia both four-wheeled and two-wheeled carts were used as mobile platforms from which soldiers could hurl spears. Solid wooden wheels made them heavy and cumbersome, but by 1900 B.C. the Mesopotamians had developed the spoked wheel—a circular outer ring supported by wooden spokes radiating from its center. This resulted in light, fast-moving vehicles that could dart about the battlefield.

ALTERNATIVES TO THE HORSE

While the horse's combination of strength and mobility made it perhaps the most versatile of the animals used by people for transportation, a number of other species are also important. In the Arctic Circle teams of dogs or reindeer are used by Eskimo peoples to pull sleds. Extreme heat and lack of water are lethal to horses, but camels thrive in such harsh environments and are vital to the desert nomads (roaming peoples) of Central Asia, North Africa, and the Middle East. A camel can carry a heavy load for 30 miles (50 km) in a single day, using only one sixth of the water that a horse would consume in a similar journey.

For really heavy work, however, there is no better animal than the elephant. In India, elephants are used to push down trees and transport logs and other heavy loads. Elephants have also been ridden into battle, where they inspired terror in opposing troops and horses. Mountainous or rocky terrain, too, can prove difficult for horses to cross, and people sought more sure-footed alternatives. The donkey is one such animal, but its small size limits the loads that it can carry, so mules, produced by breeding a male donkey with a female horse and combining the useful qualities of both animals, are often used instead.

The true mountain experts, however, are the llamas of South America and the yaks of the Himalayas, whose thick coats protect them from the cold at high altitude.

▲ Camels have a store of fat in their famous humps, which allows them to survive without eating or drinking for several days.

years ago by nomadic herders on the steppes (flat plains) of Central Asia. Riding horses gave people far greater mobility, so they could make long journeys, herd animals more easily, and tower over their enemies in battle. These early riders probably rode bareback, gripping with their knees and just using a simple strap to control their mounts. Riders placed animal skins on their horses' backs to make the ride more comfortable—so creating the first basic saddles.

Charioteers

Early domestic horses were smaller than modern breeds and not strong enough to carry heavily armed soldiers. Horse-drawn chariots made use of a horse's mobility but were stable enough to transport and fire weapons. The Hyksos people used a chariot-based army to invade the Middle East and established the Hittite Empire. In 1286 B.C. the Hyksos used 3,500 chariots to defeat the Egyptian forces of pharaoh Ramses II.

KEY COMPONENTS

Western saddle

The first horse saddle was the invention of the Scythians—a nomadic people from southern Russia who roamed through eastern Europe and the Middle East for 300 years after 600 B.C. The Scythian saddle was made of padded leather and felt and supported by hoops of birchwood. A belt around the horse's belly held it in place. These saddles gave the Scythians a much firmer seat than their bareback contemporaries, so they could use their bows more effectively in battle. The modern Western saddle—that generally used in the Americas (pictured)—shares many similarities with the Scythian design.

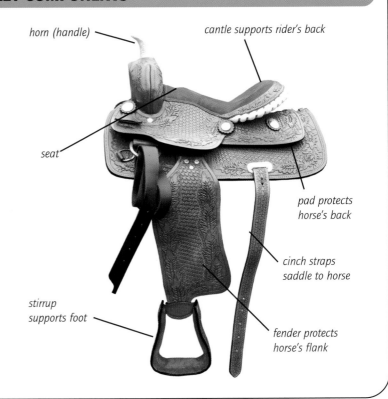

horn (handle)

cantle supports rider's back

seat

pad protects horse's back

cinch straps saddle to horse

stirrup supports foot

fender protects horse's flank

Around 1300 B.C. the Hyksos invented the bit, a piece of metal placed between the horse's teeth that can be manipulated using leather straps called reins to give commands to the horse. This remained the standard way of controlling horses until the fourth century B.C., when the Celtic tribes of northwest Europe introduced the curb bit. This is an H-shaped bit with a cross-piece in the horse's mouth. It pulls the horse's head down, giving greater control.

A new age of cavalry

Chariots were not suited for fighting in rugged terrain, so the best armies contained cavalry, warriors that rode into battle instead.

▼ Horseshoes are heated so they can be bent into the right shape before being nailed to a hoof.

The wooden-framed saddle was developed in the first and second centuries A.D. by a nomadic Central Asian people called the Sarmatians. It had arches to fit over the horse's back and high peaks front and rear so the rider was held very securely. In warfare this allowed the horseman to use a heavy weapon, such as a lance.

The Romans enjoyed chariot racing but preferred infantry (foot soldiers) for warfare. They did, however, build a remarkable network of roads and spread one important piece of horse technology, the horseshoe—a U-shaped metal plate that is nailed onto the horse's hoof to prevent it from being worn on hard surfaces.

FACTS AND FIGURES

- Modern horses are descended from the Dawn Horse, *Hyracotherium*, a tiny creature little more than 12 inches (30 cm) high that lived some 50 million years ago.
- One of the earliest known books was about horses. Written by Kikkuli, who lived in the Hittite Empire in 1400 B.C., it explained how to use horses to pull chariots.
- In the days of horse-drawn travel in the mid-19th century, there were more than a million horses stabled in London, England, and 1,000 tons (910 metric tons) of horse dung had to be cleared from the streets each day.

KEY COMPONENTS

Double bridle

Several types of bridle are used today. This shows the most complex, the double bridle, which is used for events such as dressage (horse training and maneuvering) competitions, where the rider needs extra control. Two separate bits go in the horse's mouth, each with its own set of reins. The snaffle bit, with rings at each end, goes in first. This is the bit that would be used on a single bridle and is the main aid for controlling the horse. The curb bit is H-shaped, with sides that project up and down, and a chain and strap that go behind the mouth. When the curb rein is pulled, the center of the bit presses on the mouth, while at the same time the sides are pulled backward by the reins at the bottom, making the top (eye) tilt forward. The eye pulls on the top of the horse's head through the poll strap, and on the horse's jaw through the curb chain.

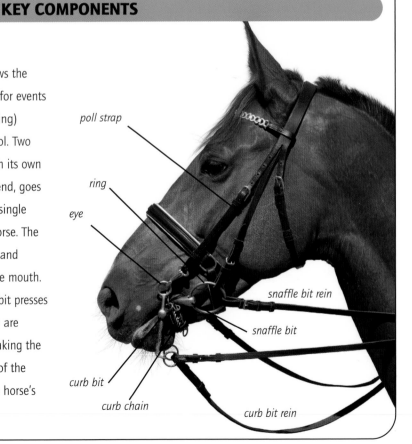

poll strap

ring

eye

snaffle bit rein

snaffle bit

curb bit

curb chain

curb bit rein

▲ *Collar harnesses put the weight of the load on the horse's shoulders rather than the neck or throat. A horse can pull four times the weight with a padded collar than it can with a primitive yoke harness.*

Carts and wagons

For most of the Middle Ages, the carts and wagons of Europe were hardly different from Roman times. Usually there were four wheels all the same size, no suspension, and no steering. The cart was just dragged around corners—even though steerable carts with pivoting front axles had been invented by the Celts around 50 B.C.

Since horses were introduced to the Middle East and Europe, various harnesses had been used, but none was ideal. They forced the horse to pull with its neck rather than its body and could easily ride up and press on its windpipe. The horse collar, a broad harness that rested over the horse's shoulders, was invented in China and allowed a wagon, plow, or canal boat to be pulled with maximum efficiency.

THE COACH

According to popular belief it was wagonbuilders in the Hungarian village of Kocs who, during the 15th century, revived the ancient idea of using small front wheels on wagons, allowing the vehicles to turn much more easily and making them more stable by placing the center of gravity farther back. Soon they added an even more important refinement, suspending the body of the vehicle between the axles rather than resting it on them—so absorbing some of the shocks of the road. The *kocsi*, or coach, was born.

▶ *Coaches spread throughout Europe in the 16th and 17th centuries. At first these high-tech and comfortable vehicles were used only by the richest families. Later larger coaches were used as long-distance public transportation.*

SCIENTIFIC PRINCIPLES

Coach suspension: mass and inertia

At first coaches were supported on leather slings, like a hammock. Then crescent-shaped metal springs called leaves were added, making a huge difference. Not only was the ride more comfortable, but the coach was much safer to drive at speed, floating over bumps rather than catapulting off them.

The springing works because the heavy carriage has so much inertia that it takes a lot of force to move it. When the coach goes over a bump, the wheels and axles go up in the air. Most of this motion is absorbed by the bending springs, and very little moves the carriage body itself. How well this works depends on how bouncy the springs are and on the ratio of the sprung weight (the body) to the unsprung weight (wheels and axles). Heavy bodies on light wheels give a smooth ride. However, wheels must be robust enough to hold the body, which also cannot be too heavy to haul forward.

Even so, wagons in 16th-century Europe struggled along at far less than walking pace. Not only were they crude constructions, but they had to run on terrible roads. The Roman roads had long since deteriorated, leaving tracks that were bumpy and dusty in summer and muddy quagmires in winter. If they could afford it, most people preferred to travel on horseback.

This changed with the invention of the coach, a comfortable design of cart that could be pulled at high speed—if the road surface

▼ *Stirrups allow a rider to stand up while on horseback, making it a lot easier to jump obstacles.*

STIRRUPS

Stirrups, light frames that support the rider's feet, were also invented in the second century A.D. They were a huge step forward in the use of horses for riding. They seated the rider more securely on the horse and reduced the level of skill required to ride at top speeds. The consequences of saddles and stirrups were still clear to see 1,000 years later in the Middle Ages. A big horse fitted with a high-peaked saddle was the preferred mount for wealthier soldiers. However, merchants, pilgrims, priests, and others could also ride on smaller horses, their feet secure in their stirrups with their goods on pack mules.

allowed it. Coaches spread throughout Europe in the 16th and 17th centuries, although only the richest families could afford this high technology—and enough horses to pull them.

However, in 1625, Londoners were offered a new service, coaches for rent, in the same way as modern taxi cabs. (The word *cab* is short for cabriolet, a small, two-wheeled horse-drawn carriage.) Later, stagecoaches also appeared—so named because they made long journeys in stages, between which the horses were rested or replaced. But it was still very costly to travel from Edinburgh to London by coach, and the roads were still so bad that most people preferred to ride. Only the coming of the Industrial Revolution, at the end of the 18th century, really spurred the demand for faster, cheaper transportation.

Turnpikes

Better roads gradually became essential during the 18th century. In France 15,000 miles (24,000 km) of new roads were built using

▼ *Before railroads were built, the quickest way to cross America was by stagecoach. In 1858, the journey from Missouri to California took 25 days.*

THE ROADBUILDERS

At the end of the 18th century roadbuilders invented new ways of making smooth roads. Two Scottish engineers, Thomas Telford (1757–1834) and John MacAdam (1756–1836) led the way. Telford's technique was to dig a trench into which he put a foundation of heavy rock topped with 6 inches (15 cm) of compacted stones. MacAdam believed in much lighter construction. He laid roads made of small stones. Workmen had to check the size of these stones with their mouths—if they were too big to fit in the mouth, they were too big for the road! His stone surface was finished by adding tar (below)—a mixture called tar-macadam, now shortened to "tarmac."

conscripted (forced) labor. In England a turnpike system was introduced. Companies were granted the right to build a section of road and in return could levy tolls from people using it. There was public anger at having to pay to use a road, and corruption was common, but the turnpike system improved the road network.

Golden age of coach travel

From the end of the 18th century roadbuilding proceeded rapidly all over Europe and the eastern part of North America. By 1830 there were 20,000 miles (32,000 km) of good roads in Britain alone. The stagecoach from London to Newcastle that once took eight days could make its journey in less than two. The age of the coach now reached its peak. Mail coaches traveled at high speeds, and many types of private carriages were developed, designed for the wealthy. In the 1840s, just as the coming of the railroads was spelling doom for the age of horse travel, horse-drawn carriages reached new heights of sophistication, with superbly constructed landaus, broughams, phaetons, victorias, and many other designs transporting people in style and comfort.

HORSES AND RAILROADS

Innovation is not a sudden process. Old and new continue to exist side by side, and new uses are often found for the old. The first railroads, for example, did not replace the horse—for they used horse-drawn cars. Long before railroad engines had been invented, horses drew loads along rail tracks. Mostly they worked in mines, hauling coal or iron ore; but the first passenger railroads were also horse drawn. The very last horse-drawn railroad service, at Fintona in Northern Ireland, operated until 1957. When steam railroads did arrive at the beginning of the 19th century, they quickly became the biggest owners of horses. Horses were used for shunting rolling stock, unloading freight cars, and taking freight on to its destination. As late as 1928 the London Midland and Scottish Railway in Britain owned over 9,600 horses.

◄ *Small, sturdy horses, known as pit ponies, were bred for hauling carts in mines.*

HUMAN POWER

In a world of high-speed cars, supersonic aircraft, and space travel it's easy to forget that most of our journeys still rely on the oldest power source—our own bodies.

Before people drove, sailed, and flew, they walked, sometimes for days on end, covering hundreds of miles. They used shoes to protect the feet. The first shoes, made 30,000 years ago during the Stone Age, were simply animal skins tied to the soles of the feet with strips of leather. In cold places the skin was pulled around the ankles for warmth. Shoes like this evolved into the moccasins that were popular

▶ The mountain bike, sometimes shortened to MTB, was invented in the 1970s.

RUBBER BOOTS

Waterproof rubber boots are known by a number of different names, from rainboots to gumboots. However, to many people they known as Wellingtons, or "wellies." This name is derived from the Anglo-Irish soldier, Arthur Wellesley, the 1st Duke of Wellington. In the early 19th century he designed a calf-length cavalry boot, made from leather, which was waterproof but also easy to fit into stirrups. Wellington's boot was also the inspiration for the cowboy boot.

▶ Rubber wellies were first manufactured in the 1850s.

▶ The Japanese geta is half sandal, half clog. During wet weather, the high "teeth" keep the foot raised above any puddles.

during the Iron Age and that were more recently used by Native Americans.

Around the world people developed shoes for different purposes, making the best use of local materials. In the desert areas of the Middle East, leather sandals were used to protect feet without making them too hot, in Europe and Japan carved wooden clogs were ideal footwear for working in muddy fields, while in China, a country with little access to leather, shoes were made of woven fabric.

▲ *Some modern houseshoes, or slippers, still use the same design as traditional animal-skin moccasins. However, modern moccasins often have a hard rubber sole.*

On your bike

Many inventors came up with plans for human-powered machines, but it wasn't until 1817 that a design came along that would lead to the bicycle of today. The German inventor Karl von Drais realized that it was possible to balance a machine on just two wheels as long as it was moving forward. His wooden Laufmaschine (running machine) had no pedals but was pushed along by the rider's feet. On a slope the rider's legs could be rested on a bar, and the machine would coast along effortlessly. Von

SLIPPING ALONG

The first skis were made about 4,500 years ago in Norway and Sweden as a way of spreading the weight of a person so that he or she didn't sink into the snow. They soon developed into an effective means of transport. Early skis were covered in animal fur arranged with the hairs pointing backward. As the ski moved forward the hair of the fur slid easily over the snow; but when skiers pushed back on the ski, the hairs would dig in to give good grip, making it possible to walk uphill. These early skiers also developed the sledge. Initially just an animal skin dragged along the ground, later versions had wooden or bone runners to reduce friction.

Modern skiing developed in the mid-19th century in Norway and then in the Alps, the mountain range that divides France, Switzerland, and Italy, when tourists began to experiment with downhill skiing. This sport became popular with the invention of the chairlift in the 1930s. Today's skis are made from carbon fiber, which is light and strong. Wax is rubbed onto the skis to fine tune them for different snow conditions and temperatures. Competition skiers choose from a large selection of waxes to get exactly the right kind of performance.

▲ *Downhill skis are bound tightly to the skier's stiff, plastic boots. This rigid connection allows the person to control the position of each ski at high speed.*

▲ A design of Karl von Drais's early pedal-free "running machine" from 1832.

Drais's invention started a craze that swept through Europe and the United States. Riding schools were set up to teach enthusiasts—mainly young men—how to ride.

Improved designs began to appear. The best was probably the Pedestrian Curricle, made by

AN OLD IDEA MADE NEW?

Time and again when people look for the earliest examples of machines that we now take for granted, the same name crops up—the Italian artist Leonardo da Vinci (1452-1519). The bicycle could be no exception. Some experts think that the first design for a bicycle was among the drawings on a da Vinci manuscript from the 1490s. However, others believe that the drawing of a two-wheeled cycle with pedals and a chain is a fake. Another curiosity is a 16th-century stained-glass window in a church in Stoke Poges, England, which appears to show an angel riding on a two-wheeled machine.

CYCLING RACES

The pedal-powered bikes, known as velocipedes, began a craze that has continued to the present day: cycling races. Riding schools opened to cater to the growing bands of new riders. The first race for velocipedes was held at Saint-Cloud Park, near Paris, on May 31, 1868, and in November of the following year a race was held over 83 miles (134 km) of public roads between Paris and Rouen. Both races were won by an Englishman called James Moore—the first successful racing cyclist. The first six-day bicycle race in the U.S. was held in Maddison Square Garden in New York City in 1891 on a board track. Today's most important cycling race—the Tour de France—began in France in 1903.

▲ Today's cycling road races may take place over many days and involve dozens of riders. The riders complete different stages of the race each day, so there are stage winners and an overall winner.

an English carriage-maker called Dennis Johnson in 1819. Better known by its nicknames, the "hobby horse" and "swift walker," Johnson's design used metal instead of wood and was lighter and better made than von Drais's original. Johnson also made a model for women, with a low frame to accommodate long dresses.

Pedal power

In 1839 Scottish blacksmith Kirkpatrick MacMillan created a hobby horse with pedals. These pedals were connected to cranks that turned the rear wheel when the pedals were pushed backward and forward. This machine was very clumsy and heavy. In the 1860s, a French invalid carriage-maker called Pierre Lallement attached pedals and cranks to the front wheel of a hobby horse. At last here was a machine—named the velocipede—that could be efficiently powered by a human.

In the 1870s, Englishman James Starley, designed the Ordinary bicycle, better known today as a "penny farthing." An Ordinary rider sat far off the ground on above a huge front

▲ This pedal-powered velocipede from the 1870s had no chain (or brakes). Instead the pedals were connected directly to the front wheel by a crank.

PENNY FARTHINGS

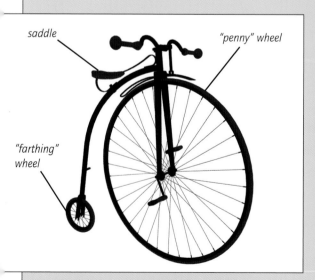

saddle

"penny" wheel

"farthing" wheel

▲ Although its real name was the Ordinary bicycle, the design was nicknamed the penny farthing because its wheels looked like large and small coins of the day.

Why was the front wheel on a penny farthing so big? The answer was speed. Cycling began as a sport, and everyone wanted to be quickest. In the days before gears were added, when pedals were attached directly to the driven wheel, the only way to make a faster bike was to fit it with a bigger wheel. With every turn a big wheel covered more ground than a small wheel. The only restriction on the size of wheel was the length of the rider's legs. The great champion of the 1880s was Herbert Lidell Cortis—a man whose height of 6 ft 2½ inches (1.89 m) allowed him to race bikes with front wheels 60 inches (152 cm) high. Modern adult-sized bikes have wheels that are generally 26 inches (66 cm) in diameter. And why was the rear wheel so small? That wheel was small to keep down the weight of the bicycle. Since the front wheel provided the drive and the steering, the rear wheel was only needed for stability.

wheel, steering with almost vertical forks. The frame of the bike was a simple tube that followed the curve of the front wheel, and attached to the back of it was a tiny rear wheel.

Despite the popularity of the Ordinary, many people found it too difficult to use. Short people could not reach the pedals, and women in their long skirts were unable to ride for fear of becoming caught in the spokes. Even the greatest supporters of the machine would often find it hard to stay balanced.

Many people tried to build safer bicycles. Chains or levers were used to gear-up a smaller front wheel so that one turn of the pedals made the wheel turn more than once. At first these

▲ *With a chain driving the rear wheels, bicycles were designed with two wheels of the same size.*

SOCIETY AND INVENTIONS

▲ *Traffic jams are rarely a problem when the roadway is filled with cyclists.*

Transport of the future

The bicycle has often seemed like a poor alternative to the car. Open to the weather, not able to hold much luggage, and usually not able to carry more than one person, bikes haven't always seemed as comfortable or as convenient as cars. This view, however, is changing. Many people are increasingly concerned about the amount of pollution and congestion brought into our cities by cars. With this concern has developed an increasing interest in healthy, more environmentally friendly modes of transportation. This is where the bike begins to look like a better option. Small in size, free of pollution, and promoting health, bicycles are now taken more seriously by many urban planners interested in improving the quality of life in cities. The result of this is an increasing number of cyclists traveling on dedicated cycling routes.

▶ *A bike chain runs from a cog wheel connected to the pedals to a series of gear cogs on the rear wheel.*

machines were ridiculed by riders of Ordinarys. But eventually the popularity of these "safety bicycles" led to the demise of the Ordinary.

The machine that changed the shape of bicycles forever was the Rover Safety, introduced in 1885 by the nephew of James Starley, John Kemp Starley. The Rover Safety set the shape of bikes as we know them today. The rear wheel

SCIENTIFIC PRINCIPLES

Derailleur gears

A bicycle's gears transmit rotary motion from the pedals to the back wheel via the bicycle chain. Derailleur gears were invented in 1911. They consist of a series of cogs attached to the drive shaft, or axle, of the rear wheel and a tension pinion that moves the chain from one cog to another. A cable connects the tension pinion to the gear controls, often a thumb switch on the handlebars or a lever on the bike frame.

To achieve maximum efficiency, the cyclist tries to keep the effort and rate of pedaling constant. On a flat surface, a high gear is selected, and the tension pinion moves the chain to a small cog. One turn of the pedals now rotates the rear wheel several times, making the bike go faster. On a hill, however, the effort required to pedal in high gear is too great, so the cyclist selects a lower gear (larger cog). The bike now moves a smaller distance for each turn of the pedals, but the effort needed to turn the pedals is smaller.

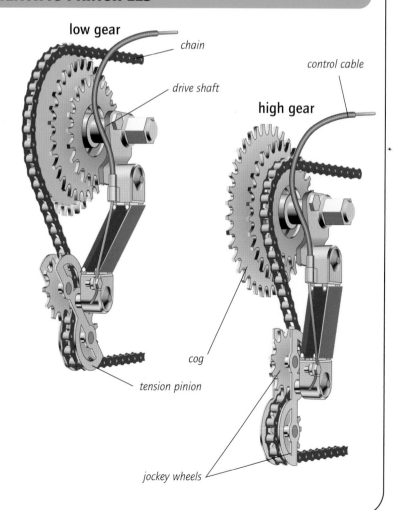

low gear
chain
control cable
drive shaft
high gear
cog
tension pinion
jockey wheels

◄ *BMX stands for bicycle motocross. BMX bikes are small and fast and used for performing aerial stunts and balancing tricks.*

was driven by a chain, and a strong frame replaced the tube of the Ordinary.

Others made their own "safetys," adding refinements. After some experimentation wheels became equal sized, the diamond-shaped frame was introduced, and finally the air-filled tires were added. These were invented in 1888 by John Boyd Dunlop (1840–1921) who fitted rubber tubes to his son's tricycle. By the 20th century, the safety was the standard bike design, and it has changed little since then.

BEST FOOT FORWARD

Although invented in the 1930s, a recumbent bicycle still turns heads on a modern street. In this design, the rider lies almost flat, peddling feet first. The recumbent bicycle is streamlined, with the rider traveling feet-first, and creates less drag than conventional bikes. The pedals are at the front of the machine, linked to the rear wheel by a long chain. The large seat and reclined riding position make this a comfortable bike, suitable for long journeys. However, the rider sits low in motor traffic, making it difficult to see—and be seen.

SUPERBIKES: THE NEED FOR SPEED

Drag force is created when an object moves through a fluid—slowing it down. In world-class sprint cycling races, high drag can make the difference between winning and losing. British cyclist Chris Boardman won a gold medal at the 1992 Olympic Games, thanks to spending many hours in a wind tunnel, perfecting his riding position. Today all top riders have superlight bikes with covered wheels and tear-drop shaped crash helmets to reduce drag.

◄ *A superbike is tested in a wind tunnel. The colored smoke shows how air moves around the speeding rider.*

Modern bikes

Although the basic shape of bicycles stays the same, many variations have been tried. For example, in 1962 British car designer Alex Moulton added a rubber suspension to a bicycle, and that made it possible to fit tiny 16-inch (40-cm) wheels highly geared to work as well as larger wheels. The rider sat high above the main frame, making it easy to get on and off, and it took up less storage space. Similar bikes have been built with folding lightweight frames, so they can be stowed inside a bag, for carrying on other modes of transport. Two hundred years after its invention, the bicycle looks here to stay.

KEY COMPONENTS

Road and trail bikes

The basic design of the bicycle has been extensively modified to suit different uses and conditions. A trail bike must be able to cope with rough terrain. It has a robust frame, with shock absorbers fitted to the front and rear forks for a smoother ride over bumps and potholes. Many uses disk brakes that act at the center of the wheel to give control over steep inclines and slippery surfaces. Racing bikes are built for speed and should only be used on roads. Lightweight frames and small caliper brakes are used to save weight. Tandem bikes are built for two riders, and have long frames.

two saddles   **Tandem**

pedals connected by chain

Trail bike

shock absorbers

thick tires

drop handlebars   **Road racer**

light frame

narrow tires

Road bikes have narrow, smooth tires that grip a flat surface while cutting drag, but are hard to steer on rough and muddy ground. Trail bikes have wide, gripped tires that work on all terrains, but do create more drag on the bike.

TRAINS AND TRACKS

Rail travel has a long history. The first tracks were built 500 years ago for hauling rocks inside underground mines. Today railroads criss-cross the world carrying passengers and freight.

The first passenger rail services were hauled by horses, but the large scale of long distance railroads demanded a mechanical source—steam engines. The first steam-powered vehicles to run on rails were built by Richard Trevithick (1771–1833), an English engineer. In February 1804 in southern Wales a locomotive he had designed pulled 5 wagons loaded with 11 tons (10 metric tons) of iron over 9.75 miles (14 km) of track at a speed of about 5 mph (8 km/h). The load also included about 70 spectators, who had climbed aboard to enjoy the ride.

◀ *Railroads have been built on many inventions. Some developed the locomotives and rail cars, while other control how trains operate safely on a busy network.*

THE FIRST RAILROADS

Railroads existed long before railroad engines did. Railroads were used in mines to move coal or iron ore. Horses, ponies, or even children were used to pull and push the wagons. Mine tracks were invented in Europe around 1550 A.D. At first the tracks were just made of wood, but later, strips of iron were fixed to the rails to keep them from wearing down too quickly. The first solid iron rails were made in England in 1738. In 1789 movable switches (points) were invented by English engineer William Jessop, allowing wagons to roll from one track to another track.

▲ *Tracks made it easier to pull loads through rough tunnels.*

Trevithick's locomotive was primitive but pointed to the future. For example, it had smooth wheels, which still gripped the rails to the surprise of many critics. It also had an efficient boiler that generated steam at high pressure. This was the breakthrough that made rail transportation possible. Previously, steam engines had been too bulky and lacked power.

The first steam engines were too heavy for the cast iron rails, which often broke. This was one reason why there was no rush to build steam railroads. Four years later Trevithick did construct a railroad to demonstrate the power of steam. His *Catch-Me-Who-Can* engine ran a circular track, and anyone who dared could ride for one shilling. But this show was a failure, and Trevithick went bankrupt.

▲ *Yellow electric streetcars have been running through Lisbon, Portugal, for almost a century.*

STREETCARS

The streetcar was invented by English engineer John Outram in 1775. His "tram" ran on rails and was drawn by two horses. In 1832, John Stephenson built the first streetcar line, again horse-drawn, in New York. It closed after three years. The main problem was that early streetcars ran on rails raised from the road that obstructed other traffic. But in 1852 French engineer Émile Loubat found a way of embedding the rails into the road surface and used this technique to build the Sixth Avenue Line in New York. Thirty years later, cities had become congested with horse-drawn traffic. Something cheaper and cleaner was needed. In 1888 U.S. engineer Frank J. Sprague built the first electric streetcar line in Richmond, Virginia. Within ten years 25,000 miles (40,000 km) of electric streetcar lines were in use in the United States.

▼ *The* Catch-Me-Who-Can *was put on show in London in Trevithick's 1808 "Steam Circus" until the heavy engine cracked the iron track, ending the exhibition.*

Great railroad pioneers

The first steam-powered locomotives started running a regular railroad railroad service on a short and narrow track between the English city of Leeds and the mining district of Middleton. The Middleton Railway had been built in 1758 to carry coal. It used horses until 1812, when a locomotive designed by English engineer John Blenkinsop (1783–1831) began to haul cargo—and occasionally passengers. Despite Trevithick's example, it ran on toothed rails, not smooth

FACTS AND FIGURES

• The standard-gauge railroad track of 4 ft 8½ in (1,435 mm) is the width of a Roman chariot's wheels. Today it accounts for about 60 percent of track worldwide.

• The widest track ever built was the 7-ft (2,134 mm) gauge developed by the British engineer Isambard Kingdom Brunel (1806–1859). He wanted extra width to give greater stability at high speed.

• Iron rails gave way to steel ones in the 19th century. In the 1950s rails were welded together into long lengths, giving a smoother ride and cheaper maintenance.

• Completed in 1916 and extending 5,750 miles (9,250 km), the Trans-Siberian Railroad is the longest continuous railroad in the world.

• The total length of railroad routes reached its peak in 1917, with about a million miles (1,600,000 km) worldwide. A quarter of the total was in the United States.

LOCOMOTIVE DESIGNS

George and Robert Stephenson were the leading locomotive designers in the early days of rail travel. Many of their decisions had a lasting impact, including the width of the gauge still used on most railroads today. Another innovation was the steam-blast design, which directed exhaust steam through a narrow blast pipe into the locomotive's chimney. Air was pulled in after the steam, increasing the draught through the furnace. This made the coal in the furnace burn hotter, increasing both the engine's power and its speed.

▶ The Stephensons show off the Rocket, the locomotive that pulled the first passenger train service in 1829.

LAYING TRACK

As well as developing locomotives and rail cars, George Stephenson established the standards to which railroads were built. He believed that the railbed should be very well prepared, the inclines (grades) should be less than one percent, so early steam engines would be able to pull long, heavy trains up them. Curves should have a radius of half a mile (0.8 km) or more to prevent derailments. His practices were followed in many countries, as foreign engineers visited England to learn about railroad construction. However, Stephenson's reliance on flat and straight tracks was unsuited to building railroads through rugged landscapes, such as in North America.

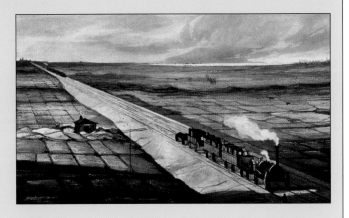

▲ *The Liverpool and Manchester Railway ran across Chat Moss Bog, bringing the latest technology to an agricultural landscape that had remained unchanged for several centuries.*

ones. But it attracted the attention of George Stephenson (1781–1848), who was convinced that he could do better.

Beginning in 1814, Stephenson built a succession of locomotives, gradually improving the design. As a result, he was made construction engineer for the Stockton and Darlington Railway. Completed in 1825, this was the first specially built steam railroad that anyone could use for shipping freight, rather than being owned and used by a single mining company. It led to a much bigger project—a railroad linking the English cities of Manchester and Liverpool. Again Stephenson supervised the line's construction, and in 1829 he won the competition for the best engine with his *Rocket* (in fact, largely designed by his son Robert, 1803–1859). This locomotive used a new and more powerful design of boiler and had a top speed of 16 mph (26 km/h) when pulling a train and 36 mph (58 km/h) on its own.

◄ *As well as passengers, the Liverpool and Manchester Railway carried livestock and heavy cargo, connecting the sea port of Liverpool with the factories of Manchester.*

Railroads in the United States

The first U.S. steam-powered passenger line, the Charleston & Hamburg Railroad, opened on Christmas Day, 1830. It ran on a 6-mile (9.6 km) stretch of track, using a U.S.-designed locomotive called the *Best Friend of Charleston*.

The railroad almost had to be reinvented for North American conditions: the long distances, high mountain ranges, extremes of climate, and sparser population. Long distances meant that railroads had to be inexpensive to build—the U.S. invention of the wooden crosstie and

▶ *A long freight train twists and turns through the Canadian Rockies.*

KEY COMPONENTS

Steam locomotive

In a steam locomotive fuel (wood, coal, or oil) is burned in a firebox directly in front of the cabin. Pipes carry the hot air and smoke from the firebox through the boiler, a large tank holding water, to the smokestack. The water starts to boil, forming steam in the dome. From the dome high-pressure steam passes to alternate sides of the cylinders, driving the pistons. Connecting rods link the pistons to the driving wheels. A safety valve allows steam to escape if the pressure becomes too great. A tender, carrying supplies of fuel and water, is coupled to the back of the engine.

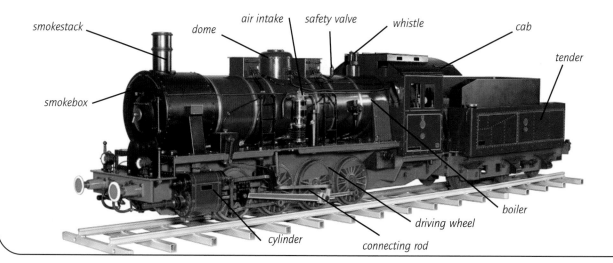

T-cross-section rail (requiring less metal than a solid rail) made this possible. Mountain crossings meant sharper curves and steeper grades. At the peak of its route over the Alleghenies, the Baltimore & Ohio Railroad climbed 1,800 ft (600 m) in a 17-mile (27 km) stretch, a grade of more than 2 percent.

Locomotives had to be designed to cope with these conditions—using the earlier British designs only resulted in frequent derailments. One early innovation was the use of a swiveling leading truck to guide the locomotive into the tighter curves. Passenger and freight cars, too, were soon built on four-wheel swiveling trucks—called bogies—rather than fixed axles. These and many other innovations produced railroads that were strong, durable, cheap to operate, and simple to maintain.

▼ *American locomotives burned wood and had a wide guard on the smokestack to prevent sparks setting forests alight. A plow-shaped cowcatcher pushed animals off the track so they did not damage the engine.*

SOCIETY AND INVENTIONS

Comfort for passengers

American railroads led the way in passenger car design. The first sleeping cars ran on Pennsylvania's Cumberland Valley Railway in 1836. Dining cars first ran in 1863, between Baltimore and Philadelphia. Two years later, U.S. industrialist George M. Pullman (1831–1897) patented his own design of sleeping car and in 1867 founded his own company, the Pullman Palace Car Company, to construct luxury passenger accommodation. Surprisingly, the scenic dome or vista dome car, so distinctive of 20th-century North American railroads, was pioneered in Russia in 1867.

cowcatcher

spark guard

two engines pull one train

SIGNALLING SYSTEMS

Modern lines use block signaling, first used by the New York & Erie Company in 1849. No train is allowed to enter a block, or section, of track until the previous train has left. The early system used colored flags and signs operated by signalmen by the track, but an automatic system was invented by Thomas Hall in 1867. One rail in each block carries a small electric current. When a train arrives in the block, the current runs through the wheels to the other rail, causing the signal to change. When the train leaves the block, the current is confined to one rail again, making the signal move to the next color setting.

1) The gray train has a green signal so the driver can travel into at least the next two blocks.

2) As the train passes the first signal, the green light turns red. The next light is yellow, warning the driver that the next one is red.

3) As the train passes the second light, it turns red. The first light turns yellow. Since another train is in the block ahead, the third light is red, signaling the driver to stop.

4) The driver passes the red by mistake, and an alarm sounds in the cab as a warning. The first light is green again since the two blocks ahead are now clear.

▲ Suburban and subway trains can get crowded. Many of the passengers travel standing up.

Subways and elevated railroads

The first subway (underground railroad) was opened in London in 1863 to ease congestion on the city streets. Its steam trains transported ten million passengers in its first year. Most subway tunnels are built by digging trenches along roads, creating a great deal of disruption for years. Elevated railroads get people off the sidewalks and can be built more easily. The first electric elevated city railroad was built in 1893 in Liverpool, England.

Replacing steam engines

The first diesel locomotive was built for Prussian State Railways in 1912. It proved a

▲ *A metro train runs along an elevated track through the Hague, Netherlands. It was built to connect older tram and train tracks in different parts of the city.*

disappointment: the mechanical transmission could not cope well with getting a heavy train underway. In the same year, however, the first diesel-electric unit was built in Sweden. It used a diesel motor to generate electricity, which

WORDS TO KNOW

- **Electromagnet:** A magnet that can be turned on and off.
- **Levitation:** To float in the air when an upward force is balancing out gravity.
- **Transmission:** The mechanism that carries the motion produced by the engine to the wheels, making them turn.

CLIMBING HILLS

Three systems have been used for getting passenger cars up steep gradients. One is the cable car in which each car is fitted with a clamp that grips a moving cable. The famous cable cars of San Francisco first ran in 1867 and were designed by Andrew Hallidie (1836–1900).

The second is the funicular railroad, which has two cars fixed to opposite ends of a cable. As one car goes up the slope, the other comes down. An engine at the top controls the cable, but little power is needed, because the two cars almost balance one another. The first funicular was built in 1879 to carry tourists up Mount Vesuvius in Italy.

Finally, the most widespread system is the rack railroad, which has interlocking teeth on the car wheels and rails. Developed by Swiss inventor Niklaus Riggenbach (1817–1899) in 1862, the original design could cope with gradients of about six percent, but later versions were built on much steeper slopes.

▲ *A funicular railroad in Zagreb, Croatia, connects the Upper Town with the city center.*

then powered the locomotive. This was the system that would eventually replace steam, since it combined high speeds with low fuel consumption and low maintenance. The world's first regular scheduled diesel-electric freight service was opened on the Santa Fe line in the United States in 1940.

Diesel engines with mechanical transmission have been used successfully in lightweight rail cars, which combine power and passenger accommodation in one unit. Some diesel-hydraulic systems have also been developed, especially in Germany. In these locomotives, the diesel engine is used to generate hydraulic (liquid) pressure, and this rotates a turbine to drive the wheels.

Modern developments

Recent inventions have centered on freight handling, safety, and high-speed trains. Highways built in the last half of the 20th century took many customers away from the railroads. Rail services fought back by introducing piggyback and container services. Carrying containers by rail meant that freight could pass from ship to train to truck without ever leaving its own container. Piggyback services carry entire road trucks with their loads of freight and are important in North America, with its vast

---

ALTERNATIVES TO STEAM

An experimental battery-powered locomotive ran in the United States in 1839. But the first really successful use of electric power was in a locomotive shown at the Berlin Fair in the summer of 1879.

Developed by German inventors Werner von Siemens and Johann Georg Malske, it proved that electric-powered trains were a practical possibility. A street railroad opened in Germany in 1881, and a small electric railroad in Ireland in 1884. The London subway system used electric locomotives in 1890.

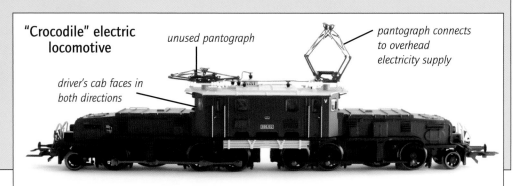

"Crocodile" electric locomotive

unused pantograph

pantograph connects to overhead electricity supply

driver's cab faces in both directions

▲ *Many commuter trains run on diesel-electric trains. The electricity generated by the engine not only drives the train but also powers doors, lights, and brakes.*

CENTRALIZED CONTROL

Block signaling is used when trains are following one another along the same track, but modern rail networks also use Centralized Traffic Control. A display in the control center shows the position of each train, and the color of every signal. Rolling-block signaling is another new innovation. There are no signals beside the track; instead, they shown in the driver's cab. This is useful on busy networks, such as subway systems.

distances. The trucks drive away from the rail terminus on to their final destinations. More recently, freight handling has been speeded by computer systems that plan the route each item should take and monitor its progress, aiming to minimize costs and maximize speed.

FACTS AND FIGURES

This table lists the countries with the ten longest railroad systems.

Country	Date	Length	Gauge
United States	1830	162,254 miles (261,124 km)	4 ft 8½ inches (1,435 mm)
Russia	1837	53,624 miles (86,300 km)	5 ft 0 inches (1,524 mm)
Canada	1836	39,487 miles (63,549 km)	4 ft 8½ inches (1,435 mm)
India	1853	38,510 miles (61,976 km	5 ft 6 inches (1,676 mm)/3 ft 3⅜ in (1,000 mm)
China	1880	33,000 miles (53,500 km)	4 ft 8½ inches (1,435 mm)
Germany	1835	25,500 miles (41,039 km)	4 ft 8½ inches (1,435 mm)
Australia	1854	24,111 miles (38,803 km)	4 ft 8½ inches (1,435 mm)/3 ft 6 in (1,067 mm)
France	1832	21,549 miles (34,680 km)	4 ft 8½ inches (1,435 mm)
Argentina	1857	21,400 miles (34,500 km)	5 ft 6 inches (1,676 mm)/3 ft 3⅜ in (1,000 mm)
Poland	1845	16,862 miles (27,137 km)	4 ft 8½ inches (1,435 mm)

KEY COMPONENTS

High-speed trains

The French electric TGVs currently holds the record for the world's fastest wheeled train. In 2007, a TGV achieved 357.2 mph (574.8 km/h). The fastest regular passenger train, the Chinese Harmony locomotive, runs at 194 mph (313 km/h). Both trains are powered by electricity, collected from overhead cables using a pantograph. This metallic arm extends upward to touch the cable and acts as a conductor, allowing electricity to pass from the cable to the train. A high-speed locomotive contains powerful electric motors that drive the wheels. Air vents keep the motors cool. The wheels are mounted on swiveling trucks, and suspension is provided by springs that ensure a smooth ride at high speeds. The typical train is made up of eight passenger cars coupled to a motor unit at each end.

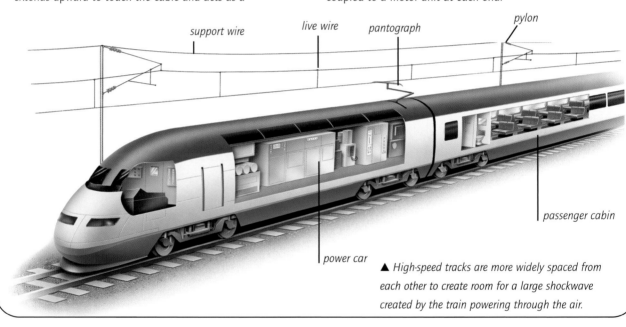

support wire   live wire   pantograph   pylon

passenger cabin

power car

▲ High-speed tracks are more widely spaced from each other to create room for a large shockwave created by the train powering through the air.

High-speed trains

Competition with short and inexpensive airline flights led to the development of high-speed trains. In 1964 the first of these, the electrically powered "bullet trains," were introduced in Japan. Japanese high-speed trains operate at speeds of 160 mph (257 km/h).

In France gas-turbine engines were developed for use in locomotives. These use hot gases turning turbines to generate electric power (or sometimes drive the wheels directly), but oil price increases made them uneconomic. In the end the important French innovation has been the electric TGV (Train à Grande Vitesse)—a permanently coupled, lightweight train, running on a specially built track.

Maglevs

A train running on a single central rail is called a monorail. Monorail maglev trains are currently

the fastest type of locomotive. Maglev stands for magnetic levitation. The trains have no wheels but float above the track—and so achieve great speed. The fastest train on record is a Japanese maglev, which managed 361 mph (581 km/h) in 2003. The trains are very expensive and there are still only a few maglev passenger services.

▶ *A high-speed maglev train connects Shanghai, China, with the city's main airport.*

SCIENTIFIC PRINCIPLES

Maglev system

1. Suspension Electromagnets, fixed to the outside of the train, are positioned so they lie underneath the track's suspension rails. When the power is on, the electromagnets are attracted upward toward the rails but are not quite powerful enough to reach them, because of the train's weight. This lifts the train, so it floats around the track.

2. Propulsion A linear motor is fitted along the underside of the train. It consists of a line of magnets (linear motor coils) that can switch between poles (shown as red and blue). The magnets are switched back and forth, creating a surge of magnetic field flowing along the train's length. This produces another magnetic field in the reaction rail that runs along the center of the track. The two fluctuating magnetic fields push and pull against each other, forcing the train along.

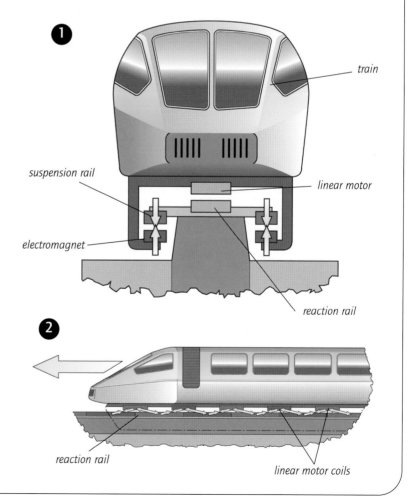

❶
train
suspension rail
linear motor
electromagnet
reaction rail

❷
reaction rail
linear motor coils

ON THE ROAD

Gasoline-driven vehicles took to the road more than 100 years ago. But the very first road vehicles had appeared long before that. What set them apart was that they were driven by steam.

The world's first self-propelled road vehicle was a steam carriage was built in France in 1769 by Nicholas Joseph Cugnot. His immense vehicle had mixed success, and steam engineers focused on building railroad locomotives or powerful stationary engines. However, Cugnot's carriage inspired others to develop steam engines small enough to fit into a road vehicle. In the United States, two New Englanders, Nathan Read and Apollo Kinsley, both ran steam vehicles in the 1790s. By 1800, there were steam buses in Paris—but only for a short time. In England a Cornish mining engineer, Richard Trevithick, built a machine with driving

PUBLIC TRANSPORTATION

Walter Hancock tried to use the new steam carriage to challenge the supremacy of horse-drawn omnibuses on the streets of London. Beginning in 1831, he built nine impressive machines, culminating in a 22-seater capable of 20 mph (32 km/h). But road toll charges for steam-powered vehicles increased, and by 1836 he had been driven out of business.

▼ *An 1801 steam cab had room for just four passengers but was considerably larger than its horse-drawn competitors.*

◄ *Modern road networks allow drivers to go where they want, whenever the want. Traffic jams result when everyone wants to go to the same place at the same time.*

wheels 10 ft (3 m) in diameter. But it was broken up when Trevithick decided that railroads were a better prospect as the transportation of the future.

Later, steam did reappear on city streets. The first practical steam truck worked in Glasgow, Scotland, in the 1870s. Steam delivery trucks started operating in Paris in 1892. Steam trucks were used by some breweries and coal merchants right through to the 1920s. But it was in the countryside—in agriculture and heavy traction—that steam power really made its mark in the form of early tractors. In the later 19th century they became a familiar sight, pulling and powering early farm machinery, especially on the flat prairies of North America. In many countries steam tractors became a feature of the large traveling circuses of the time. The vehicles hauled the showmen's wagons by day and then drove carousels at night.

CUGNOT'S STEAM CARRIAGE

Early steam engines were huge and mainly designed for pumping water out of mines—far too big to use for transportation. But eventually, in 1769, a French military engineer called Nicholas Joseph Cugnot (1725-1804) succeeded in building a three-wheeled carriage, which was demonstrated in Paris. Traveling at less than walking speed, it crashed into a wall and then ran out of steam after just 15 minutes. Even so, the authorities ordered an improved version to pull cannons—but then never put it to any use.

▼ *The boiler on Cugnot's carriage was a large metal vessel at the front. It was this part of the vehicle that crashed into a wall during the world's first automobile accident.*

Benz builds a car

While Daimler put his prototype engine into a motorcycle, another German pioneer decided to use a tricycle. In doing so he made what is now generally accepted as the first real automobile. That man's name was Karl Benz (1844–1929).

Like Daimler, Benz began as a maker of stationary gas engines. His advanced designs proved very successful, and his business was thriving, so it was a shock to his associates when he announced that he wanted to put money into building a motor vehicle. But Benz was determined and soon converted one of his engines to run on benzene—all he needed now

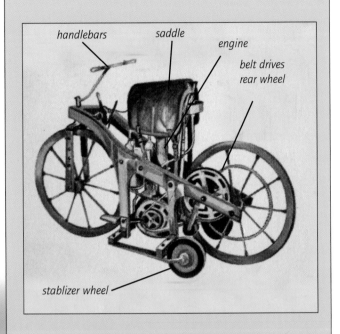

▼ *Steam tractors, complete with smokestack, resembled small rail locomotives, although with only four wheels.*

DAIMLER MOTORCYCLE

In the 1860s and 1870s, as steam engines became smaller and lighter, lightweight steam cars were designed in a number of countries. One experiment in 1868 even used a simple velocipede bicycle of the time in an attempt to make a steam motorcycle. But the true ancestor of the modern motorcycle was built in 1885 by Gottlieb Daimler (1834–1900). Throughout the 19th century, inventors had been working toward an effective internal-combustion engine. Daimler built a benzene-powered engine and needed a vehicle to test it on. He constructed a crude, wooden-framed motorcycle that anticipated later designs in having the engine mounted in the middle and driving the rear wheel. But he also added small outrigger wheels that could be lowered to keep the machine on an even keel. With no suspension and tireless steel-rimmed wheels, riding it must have been a difficult and exciting experience. Daimler soon abandoned the motorcycle and turned his attention to the automobile—with much greater success.

KEY COMPONENTS

The early automobile

The first automobiles owed a great deal to the horse-drawn carriage. In fact, many were simply coaches with an engine—one reason why they were known as "horseless carriages." Even specially built cars were usually made by traditional coachbuilders and so had the same large wheels, distinctive body, and high driver's seat. Light wheels and slow speed meant that the first cars could be steered with a small tiller on an upright column in the middle of the car. The engine settings had to be adjusted constantly using levers on the steering column or a control nearby. Speed was controlled by moving a lever back and forth. There was no brake pedal in the early car, just a hand brake that clamped brake pads against the wheel rims (like modern bicycle brakes) or pulled a belt tight around the axle. Weaker drivers could not pull on the brake lever hard enough to stop a speeding car. The first motor vehicles often jolted along on spoked bicycle wheels or on heavy wheels adapted from carts with wooden spokes and solid rubber rims. By 1895 many were beginning to use air-filled pneumatic tires, but punctures were frequent. The first pressed steel wheel was introduced in 1910. When turning corners, the outer wheel must turn much faster than the inner, and a differential gear on the rear axle was in use as early as Benz's two-seater tricycle of 1885. In many early cars the power of the engine was transmitted to the wheels by a chain or even a leather belt. But in 1895, the Renault company championed the idea of a rigid metal drive shaft linked to universal joints through which power can be passed in any direction. This system is still used today.

Benz Tricycle, 1886

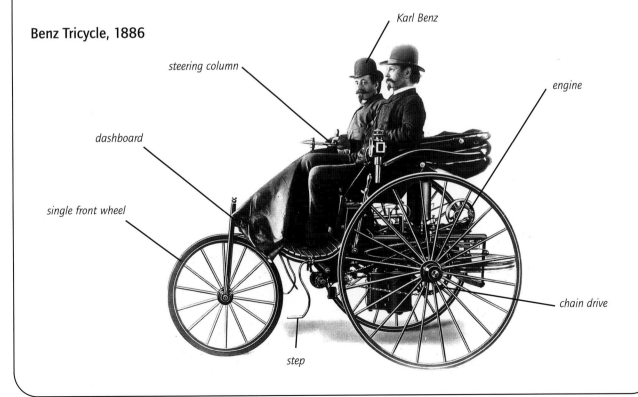

Karl Benz

steering column

engine

dashboard

single front wheel

chain drive

step

WHO INVENTED THE AUTOMOBILE?

People have argued long and hard over who invented the automobile. Some say it was the Belgian Étienne Lenoir, who drove a gas-engined carriage as early as 1862 and even sold one to the Czar of Russia. Some argue for the Austrian Siegfried Marcus, who fitted an engine to a handcart in about 1870. Another contender is Frenchman Edouard Delamere-Deboutteville, who in 1883 tried putting a gasoline engine into two different chassis, but both proved too fragile. But it was the German engineer Karl Benz (1844–1929) who was the first man to build a vehicle with an internal-combustion engine and turn it into a practical commercial proposition.

▲ Many early cars were built in France by companies, such as Peugeot and Renault, that still produce them today.

was a vehicle to put it in. He decided that three wheels would give both stability and simplicity, and he drew on cycle technology to keep down the weight.

The result, in 1886, was a spindly machine, which gave little consideration to comfort but worked very well and was reliable, so long journeys were possible. Benz improved the design and began to sell his automobiles to the public. This was the birth of the motor industry.

Rapid progress

Automobile production quickly spread to other countries, and design developed rapidly. The year 1895 was a particular turning point. The first automobile with fully enclosed engine and body appeared: a Panhard-Levassor, built in France. The first brake shoe was developed, and the first direct driveshaft transmission system was designed in the same year.

TIRE LEADER

The first automobile to be fitted with pneumatic tires—a Peugeot with a four horsepower Daimler engine—competed in the Paris-Bordeaux race of 1895. The tires had to be changed 22 times in the course of the 750-mile (1,200 km) race—even though each tire was fitted to its wheel with 20 nuts and bolts! The driver, Edouard Michelin, went on to found the well-known Michelin tire company.

◄ Cars should carry a jack, a simple lifting device used to raise the tire off the ground so it can be changed when it is damaged.

KEY COMPONENTS

Motorcycle

This racing superbike is the pinnacle of motorbike design. Electronic ignition starts the engine; older models were kick started. The engine is a smaller version of a car engine, with cylinders inside which fuel is burned pushing pistons down. These, in turn, rotate a crankshaft. A chain drive transmits the power of the engine via a gearbox to the back wheel. The engine is cooled by liquid that circulates around the cylinders and through a radiator, where air is drawn in to cool the liquid. Burned gases pass out through the exhaust.

The rider uses hand and foot levers to brake, a twist-grip on the right handlebar (throttle) controls the engine's speed, and one on the left handlebar controls the clutch (which engages or disengages the engine from the transmission system). The brakes are disk brakes. The rider wears a suit made from tough leather with extra protection on the back in case of an accident. The suit will allow him or her to slide over the ground and slow down gradually—hopefully avoiding injuries. A helmet protects the head.

windshield

disk brakes

leathers

chain drive

FACTS AND FIGURES

- When automobiles first appeared in the United Kingdom they were treated under the same laws as steam traction engines, which meant that, officially, someone had to walk in front carrying a red flag!

- The modern automobile's dashboard, or instrument panel, got its name because on horse-drawn carriages there was a board in front of the coachman to stop him being dashed by stones thrown up by the horses' hooves.

- The first automobile to be used in an election campaign was the Mueller-Benz lent to the Democratic presidential candidate William Jennings Bryan, on his visit to Decatur, Illinois, in October 1896.

- By 1913 the United States had already become the first country to have more than a million automobiles. The current figure is about 244 million: one for every 1.2 people.

Commercial vehicles also appeared in 1895. The first gasoline-driven motor bus went into service, over a 9-mile (15 km) route in North Rhineland, Germany; the first gasoline-engined van was put into production; and the first prototype gasoline-engined truck, also a Panhard, was tried out in Paris.

Other improvements soon followed: glass windshields in 1903, fenders in 1905, and rearview mirrors in 1906. But private cars were still expensive hobbies for the wealthy. It took Henry Ford's assembly line to change that.

From hand levers to disk brakes

Thousands of small inventions continued to make automobiles more powerful, more comfortable, and easier to control. Brakes, for example, have changed dramatically from the earliest examples. The earliest cars had no brake pedal, only a parking brake lever. The brakes themselves were usually just pads that pressed

▼ *On modern production lines, cars bodies are assembled largely by robots. Later, human workers fit the engine and many smaller components to the vehicle.*

HENRY FORD AND THE MODEL T

Businessman Henry Ford (1863–1947) set up his Ford Motor Company in June 1903. At first he built his cars in the usual costly way, as individual hand-built items. The total world output of cars in that year was under 62,000 vehicles— almost half of them built in France.

Then in 1908 Ford introduced the revolutionary approach that was to make his name: a standardized car, the famous Model T; simplified spare parts; and, to keep costs down, a routinized production line on which each worker performed preset tasks as the vehicles being assembled moved by on a conveyor belt. Between 1908 and 1927, 15 million Model T Fords were built—the equivalent of over 14,000 a week! By 1920 half the cars in the world were Fords.

▲ Henry Ford famously said, "Any customer can have a car painted any color that he wants, so long as it is black."

SOCIETY AND INVENTIONS

▲ The cloverleaf interchange, in which drivers can move from one highway to another without stopping, was invented by American engineer Arthur Hale in 1916. Interchanges such as this take up a lot of space but allow cars to keep moving.

Driving society

The motor vehicle has been one of the greatest forces for change in the 20th century. The mobility it allows has affected every aspect of people's lives: where they live, where they work, where they shop, where they go for entertainment. The result has generally been far greater choice and freedom. But a more mobile society has also perhaps meant less community spirit. It has also meant that our surroundings have become more compartmentalized: separate areas for living, areas for working, areas for shopping, and so on. At the same time, the needs of the automobile have changed our surroundings: more and more roads, increased traffic, more and more parking, and more and more pollution caused by the burning of gasoline and diesel.

◀ *The disk brake is seen clearly in this cut-through tire.*
▼ *Many high-performing sports cars have their brakes on show inside the wheel.*

on the rim of the wheel. Whether the brakes actually stopped the vehicle depended on the strength of the driver. By the early 1900s foot-operated drum brakes were the standard system. The brake pads were semicircular brake shoes, hidden in a drum fixed to the inside of each wheel. The drums helped keep off rain and mud, and there was some leverage to help the driver. But the brakes still needed regular adjusting to maintain equal pressure on each wheel.

By the 1930s automobiles were becoming much faster and heavier: drivers needed more assistance. Hydraulic brake systems were invented. The brake pedal and brakes were linked by tubes filled with oil instead of metal cables. But by the 1950s cars' speeds and weights had overtaken the system again. So

THE BEETLE

The Volkswagen Beetle, one of the world's most recognizable and popular automobiles, has had a checkered past. In 1938 the Nazi leader Adolf Hitler launched the Volkswagen VW—the "People's Car"—a low-cost mass-produced car designed for ordinary drivers. The VW was designed by Ferdinand Porsche (1875-1951), and the VW company was set up by the government. At the same time, the Nazis were developing Germany's autobahn system—a network of roads that became a model for modern expressways. After World War II a U.S. advertising campaign gave the car the nickname "Beetle" because of its unusual rounded shape and small size.

▲ *The original design of the Beetle is no longer made, but these cars are still maintained—and raced—by fans.*

THE ABS SYSTEM

The natural reaction in an emergency is to put the foot firmly on the brake pedal and keep it there. This can make the wheels lock and the automobile skid. It will stop—but a vehicle slows best when its tires are gripping the road, so friction between tire and road is high. As soon as the wheel skids, that grip is lost. In the 1970s the Bosch company of Germany developed ABS (Antilock Braking System) to solve this problem. ABS uses sensors on each wheel, sending information to a computer. When a locked wheel is detected, the computer can release and re-activate the brakes up to 15 times a second to prevent a skid. The driver can still steer the braking vehicle, making it possible to drive around obstructions.

SCIENTIFIC PRINCIPLES

Braking pressure

A car's brake pedal is linked to the brakes by pipes filled with oil. Pressing down on the pedal moves a piston that puts pressure on the oil, and this pressure passes to the brakes. This system instantly puts equal pressure on left and right brakes, thanks to the principles of hydraulics—the laws about the behavior of fluids. When a liquid is in a closed container, the pressure throughout the liquid is always equal. So if you press a liquid at one end, the force immediately passes to the other. Since a car's brakes are interconnected, they form one "container," so the pressure on each side is always the same.

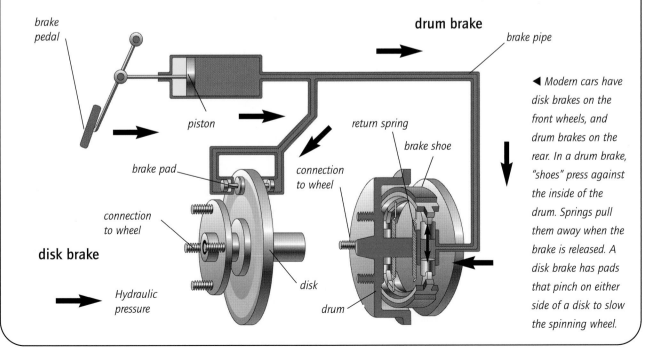

brake pedal

drum brake

brake pipe

piston

return spring

brake shoe

brake pad

connection to wheel

connection to wheel

disk brake

disk

Hydraulic pressure

drum

◀ Modern cars have disk brakes on the front wheels, and drum brakes on the rear. In a drum brake, "shoes" press against the inside of the drum. Springs pull them away when the brake is released. A disk brake has pads that pinch on either side of a disk to slow the spinning wheel.

technology that prevents wheelspin when accelerating. But perhaps more of the future may be glimpsed by looking at racing cars.

High-tech racing

In the 1990s international Formula One racing cars reached a peak of technical sophistication. They had ABS and traction control, and computer technology also allowed many other functions to be taken out of the driver's hands. A totally automatic transmission insured that

▲ *Formula One cars move at almost 200 mph (320 km/h) during a race. At this speed they would take off if it were not for an upside-down wing at the back, which pushes the car back down on to the track.*

power-braking came in: still hydraulic, but with a vacuum system providing the power, not just the force applied to the brake pedal.

Finally, in the 1970s disk brakes began replacing drum brakes—usually just on the front wheels, with drums still on the rear. Disk brakes had been invented back in 1902, only they were expensive to make. But they were more dependable and could no longer be ignored.

The future

ABS brings us to the present and future of automobile innovation—for it was the first major invention made possible by putting computers into cars. Two things especially seem likely to change motor vehicles in the future. One is new sources of power: electric batteries or fuel cells. The other is on-board computers. Already, most cars have traction control, another computerized

ALTERNATIVE POWER

As the cost of drilling for oil rises and the links between burning fuels and climate change become more obvious, automobile manufacturers are looking to alternative fuels. Hydrogen is a possibility. When hydrogen burns, it combines with oxygen

▲ *Electric cars just need to be plugged in, although the recharging process can take several hours.*

in the air to create water vapor. Hydrogen cars have been tested, but the gas is hard to handle safely, making fueling hydrogen cars potentially dangerous. Another alternative is the electric car, powered by rechargeable batteries. Many of the electric-powered cars on the road today are hybrids. They use both gasoline and electric motors. Electricity powers the car at low speeds, while the gasoline engine kicks in at higher speeds when it is most efficient.

THE JEEP

The jeep is one of the best known motor vehicles in the world. Yet, 60 years ago it was hurriedly put together from bits of other vehicles, designed by three separate teams. In June 1940 the U.S. government invited 135 motor manufacturers to design a new small, general-purpose automobile for the army. They received proposals from just two: the American Bantam automobile Co. and Willys-Overland. Both small firms, they were looking for business while their bigger rivals were busy supplying a growing automobile market. But at the army's insistence they were soon joined by a serious competitor—the Ford Motor Co. American Bantam was first to complete a prototype—the basic design took just five days. All three firms used whatever components were readily available. Engines, instruments, gearboxes, and transmissions were taken from cars, trucks, even tractors. As for the name, the prototypes were called the Bantam Field Car, Willys Quad, and Ford

Pygmy. But then Ford changed their name to "GP," for General Purpose. "GP" soon changed to "jeep," and the name stuck. Following trials, it was decided to order the Willys version in large numbers, but with the front end of the Ford grafted on. Ford agreed to build it in their huge factories. Unlike other cars, a jeep's engine turned all four wheels, allowing it to drive "off-road" up hills and through slippery mud. The large wheels raised the body high above any obstructions. The jeep went on to become the workhorse of the Allied armies. Some jeeps were lengthened, others shortened, some became ambulances, half-tracks, or versions called "seeps" that traveled through water. One prototype was even fitted with rotor blades so it could fly into battle towed behind an airplane! A modern jeep is called an SUV (Sports Utility Vehicle, below). SUVs are no longer specialist military vehicles, but used for everything from carrying groceries from the store to driving through a jungle.

the vehicle was always in exactly the correct gear for every part of the circuit. Computerized controls replaced the traditional accelerator. Hydraulic rams constantly adjusted the suspension to improve grip and cornering. Four-wheel steering (the rear wheels turning as well as the front) helped improve stability.

In addition the on-board computer stored information from every lap of the circuit. If a driver thought that a particular lap was perfect, it could be copied, with the computer making sure that every gear change, throttle movement, acceleration, braking force, and suspension movement would be exactly the same for the rest of the race.

These high-tech cars took the fun and excitement out of racing and are now banned from competitions. Racing round a track is hardly the same as making an everyday journey, but such developments give an idea of what the automobile of the future might be like.

▲ A Segway is an electric vehicle controlled by a gyroscope. When the rider leans forward slightly, the vehicle moves forward. Leaning back slows the Segway to a stop.

PUTTING DRIVERS IN THE PICTURE

Today most automobiles boast an impressive array of high-tech electronics and computerized control systems. In recent years, for example, driver information display has been quietly revolutionized by digital technology, such as satellite navigation maps. Analog (clock dial) displays have been retained for the speedometer, fuel levels, and rev (engine revolution) counter because drivers find it easier to take in changing analog information at a glance. Other functions, such as the stereo, heating, and air conditioning are controlled from a single touchscreen.

◄ Satellite navigation systems pick up signals from satellites to calculate the car's position. A computer then calculates the best route to the destination.

Rally car

This Toyota Corolla rally car races over long distances and rough terrain. A battery behind the co-driver's seat supplies electricity to start the four-stroke engine as well as powering electronic systems such as windshield wipers, lights, and the fuel-injection system. When the accelerator pedal is pressed, the fuel-injector mixes fuel with air and pumps it under pressure directly into the engine block's cylinders. Sparks ignite the fuel, and the pistons start pumping up and down in the cylinders. Connecting rods turn a crankshaft, which transmits energy to the vehicle's transmission, which turns the wheels around. The transmission includes gears that vary the speed and torque of the engine. The gears are changed by hydraulic shift. The engine's power is increased by a turbocharger—a turbine driven by exhaust gases. Burned gases escape from the exhaust system—most vehicles are fitted with catalytic convertors that break down most of the harmful pollutants that would otherwise be let out of the exhaust. The engine is cooled by water. The water circulates around the cylinders and then sheds heat through the radiator.

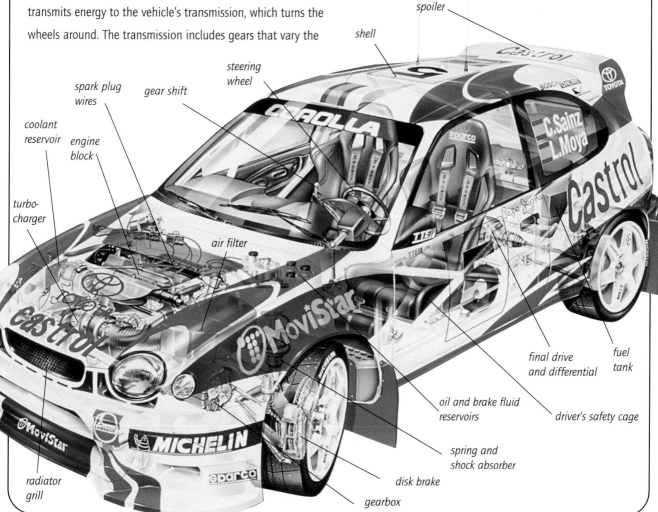

SHIPS AND BOATS

People have traveled by boat for thousands of years, and boats have played a crucial role in the spread of civilizations throughout history. Today's ships are the largest forms of transportation ever made.

We have no real way of knowing when boats were first used. But we do know that Aboriginal people used boast to reach Australia at least 50,000 years ago, and other people spread through the Pacific islands around the same time. So they must have had ocean-going craft as long ago as this. The first people to arrive in the Americas about 14,000 years ago probably traveled by sea down the west coast, which was covered in ice at the time.

DUGOUTS

The oldest remains of boats are just 8,000 or so years old, like the 13-foot (4 m) canoe found at Pesse, Netherlands. Like many boats dating from this time—and many boats even today—this canoe was simply a hollowed-out log.

▲ *A simple canoe cut from a tree trunk.*

▶ A replica Greek trireme is tested on the waters of the Aegean Sea. The ship is powered by 170 oars and has a top speed of about 9 mph (14 km/h). Speeding triremes were used to ram enemy ships in battle.

Skin and bark

Ancient people would have seen logs floating down rivers and used them to make rafts—and then dugout canoes. Canoes were also made by stretching animal skins over a light frame of bent wood and bound together with strips of leather. A skin canoe dating from around 4500 B.C. was found on the Baltic island of Fünen. Skin canoes are much lighter than dugouts, are easier to handle, and can cope with surprisingly rough water. They can often be carried from river to river by a single person.

One fascinating boat of this kind is the quffa used on the Tigris and Euphrates rivers in Iraq and dating back many thousands of years. Quffa are round canoes up to 18 ft (5.5 m) across and able to carry up to 20 passengers. They are made by sealing basketwork with tar.

Right across the world, from Australia to North America, people learned how to make canoes from tree bark sewn together with tree roots and sealed with tree resin, and these bark canoes proved both light and strong. The Native American Algonquins and Iroquois both made canoes from tree bark. The Algonquins used white paper birch bark, and this proved the best material, but the Iroquois used elm bark. Other tribes used chestnut and even spruce. These bark canoes were the inspiration for today's sport canoes of fiberglass and plastic.

PLANK BOATS

By lashing planks together, boats can be built much bigger than either a dugout from a single tree or a skin canoe. In 2000 B.C. the shipbuilders of ancient Egypt were making ships over 100 ft (30 m) long by interlocking 1,000 or more small planks of wood and lashing them together with tough grass rope. By 1000 B.C. the traders of Phoenicia (now Lebanon) were venturing out of the Mediterranean and braving the vast open spaces of the Atlantic in stout sea-going ships made from long planks of cedar, held together with wooden ribs.

Planking—which could be either edge-joined or overlapped—not only made it possible to make big, light, seaworthy ships, it also allowed boats to be shaped so that they cut smoothly and swiftly through the water. Nowhere was this demonstrated more clearly than in the long, low, elegantly shaped longships made over 1,000 years ago by the Vikings, which carried them from Scandinavia to Britain, Iceland, and Greenland, and even to North America, where a few settled in what they called Vinland (modern-day Newfoundland).

Sail power

All the earliest craft were driven along by hand—either a pole pushed along the bottom or a paddle dipped into the water. But sails exploiting the power of the wind were probably first used about 7,000 years ago in Mesopotamia, in modern Iraq, on trading boats made of reeds. The first known picture of a sail dates from 3500 B.C. and comes from Egypt. The sail is simply a large square of cloth hung from a spar (the yard pole) mounted on a mast.

The earliest sailing boats had square sails and depended on a following wind. But by

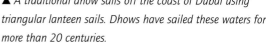

▲ A traditional dhow sails off the coast of Dubai using triangular lanteen sails. Dhows have sailed these waters for more than 20 centuries.

▼ A sloop is a small sail boat. It has two triangular sails and can be controlled by just one person. Sloops are only suitable for sailing close to land.

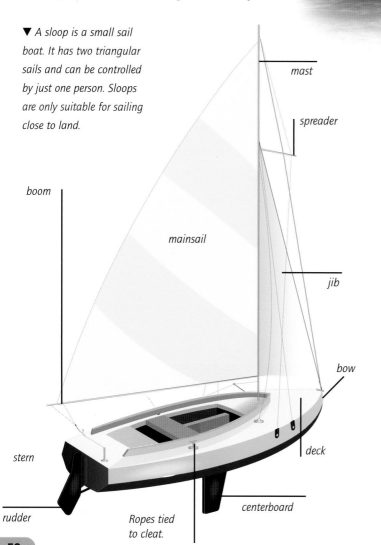

- mast
- spreader
- boom
- mainsail
- jib
- bow
- deck
- stern
- rudder
- centerboard
- Ropes tied to cleat.

SCIENTIFIC PRINCIPLES

How boats sail against the wind

Sailing ships can sail against the wind because when sailing in that direction the wind does not push the sail so much as suck it. The sail acts like an airfoil (the shape of an aircraft wing). As the wind blows over the curve of the sail, it speeds up and the pressure drops on that side, creating a lift force—just as above an wing. This force pulls the boat forward. By zigzagging at the right angle, first one way then the other—a technique called tacking—a boat can make headway almost directly into the wind. Some modern yachts can sail as close as 39 degrees to the angle of the wind (0 degrees is straight into the wind).

Clippers and tall ships

The pinnacle of sailing ship technology, perhaps, was reached in the clippers of the 1800s, which were first made in the United States. These ships got their name because they tried to "clip" time off as they raced to get their cargoes of Chinese and Indian tea first on the market in Europe and America. Designers shaved down the hull to a sleek minimum and mounted huge areas of sail on tall masts to make the most of the wind. Clippers like these could reach speeds of well over 30 knots (35 mph, or 56 km/h). In 1866 the clippers *Taeping*, *Serica*, and *Ariel* raced 15,970 miles (25,700 km) from Fuzhou in southern China to London in just 99 days.

Like other tall ships, clippers consisted of a complex combination of square sails and triangular lanteen sails. The sails were made for canvas (heavy cotton). Square sails were hung across the width of the ship from crossbars, known as yardarms. The square sails could pivot on horizontal booms to take maximum advantage of different wind directions. The lanteen sails were hung along the length of the ship and were there to pick up cross winds on either their front or back surface. This arrangement permitted clippers to sail almost into the wind, which meant they were less at the mercy of the wind direction. Their huge area of sail also allowed them to take advantage of even the gentlest breezes.

▲ *Tall ships—so called because of their tall masts, which are almost as high as the ship is long— still sail the oceans today. Many are used as training vessels for young naval cadets to "learn the ropes"—the basics of sailing.*

▲ *Most of the rudder is under the water. It is a flat board that can move from side to side. When moved to the side, the rudder pushes on the water flowing past. In response, the water pushes against the boat, changing its direction.*

A.D. 200 sailors in the Mediterranean were using triangular lanteen sails, much like those used on Arab dhows, which were better at sailing into the wind.

Ocean going vessels

For 1,000 years or more the merchants' ships changed little. They were steered by an oar over the side and rarely had more than two sails. But around 1200 the steering oar was replaced on European ships by a hinged rudder over the stern (the rear of the boat). This old Chinese invention made the boat much more maneuverable, allowing progress even when the wind was against you. A mixture of square and lanteen sails meant boats could sail with winds

STEAM POWER

▲ *Robert Fulton with his riverboat* Clermont *behind.*

In the late 1700s sails were becoming old technology. In 1783, the Marquis d'Abbans ran a steam-powered boat on the Saône River in France. Four years later Englishman John Wilkinson (1728–1808) proved an iron boat could float on the Severn River.

By 1801, William Symington (1763–1831) had launched the world's first steamship, the *Charlotte Dundas*, on the Forth and Clyde Canal. A few years later American Robert Fulton set up the first regular steamship service on the Hudson River. Then in 1819, the steam-powered *Savannah* crossed the Atlantic, though it relied on sails for most of the journey.

LIGHTHOUSES

Before the invention of lighthouses, large fires were burned on hilltops to warn ships of treacherous rocks. The earliest known lighthouse was the Pharos of Alexandria in Egypt. Built around 280 B.C. by Sosastros of Cnidus, this structure stood some 350 ft (110 m) high. Its construction was a remarkable achievement at the time and provided the model for all later lighthouses. The 18th century saw the development of the modern lighthouse. In 1759 a lighthouse made of interlocking stone blocks was built on the Eddystone Rocks reef in England. Designed by the English engineer John Smeaton (1724–1792), this was a breakthrough in making lighthouses more resistant to the damage caused by the power of the sea. In the 20th century concrete and steel have taken over from stone, while modern navigation technology has reduced the need for lighthouses, and the remaining few have mostly been automated.

from almost any direction. By the 15th century European explorers were using light, fast, highly maneuverable sailing boats called caravels to make epic voyages of discovery.

Propeller power

The early steamships were driven along by paddle wheels positioned on either side of the hull or, on most Mississippi steamboats, the stern (the rear of the boat). Paddle wheels were simple, but they were vulnerable to damage and inefficient, since the paddle was out of the water for much of the time.

Many people believed the answer was a screw propeller. This idea dated back to the ancient Greek philosopher Archimedes, who

▼ A paddlesteamer sails into the modern port of Savannah, Georgia. 150 years ago, this river boat would have been the fastest vessel around.

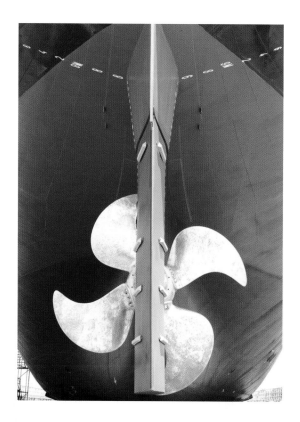

developed a device like a corkscrew in a tube to lift water from rivers. But it was not until 1836 that Francis Smith in England and John Ericsson in Sweden finally came up with a successful design for a screw propeller. This proved a crucial breakthrough. In 1845 a tug-of-war was

◄ *The shape of a ship's propeller, or screw, makes it force water backward as it turns. The water pushes back, creating a thrust force that moves even giant ships forward.*

held between a paddle steamer and a screw-driven steamship. The screw-driven ship won easily, pulling the paddle steamer backward through the water.

Steel construction

For most of the last half of the 19th century, the largest ships were built from iron. However, in 1900, steel replaced iron to make ships stronger and lighter, and hull plates began to be welded together, not riveted. The introduction of watertight bulkheads, separating the hull into sections, reduced the chances of water flooding the hull even if a leak did develop.

Around the same time, ships began to use the steam turbine engines developed by Sir Charles Parsons toward the end of the 19th century. In a turbine engine, the flow of hot steam from the boiler spins propeller-like blades

IRON SHIPS

There was a limit to the size of boats made of wood, both because large pieces of wood, or timbers, were scarce and because wood was simply not strong enough for boats much longer than 300 feet (90 m). Isambard Kingdom Brunel (1806–1859) built two great ships of iron—the *Great Britain* (1843) and the *Great Eastern* (1858), and since then metal ships driven by screws have been built steadily bigger and bigger.

SOCIETY AND INVENTIONS

Disasters at sea

On April 14–15, 1912, the *Titanic*, then the world's largest passenger liner, sank 400 miles (640 km) off the coast of Newfoundland. 1,515 people died. The ship had been designed with a double-bottomed hull, which was divided into 16 watertight compartments. It was possible for four of these compartments to be flooded without the ship sinking. Shortly before midnight on April 14, the *Titanic* hit an iceberg, causing five of the watertight compartments to be flooded. Two hours later the ship sank. It was later found that there were lifeboats for only half the passengers, and hundreds of people died in the cold water.

Disaster has also struck cargo ships, and one of the most famous of these was the oil tanker *Exxon Valdez*. On March 24, 1989, this tanker ran aground on Bligh Reef off the coast of Alaska. Instructions to change course were not properly carried out. It is estimated that over 11 million gallons (50 million liters) of oil were released, polluting an area of 500 square miles (1,200 sq km).

▶ *The* Lusitania, *a luxury liner with 2,000 people aboard, sunk off the coast of Ireland in 1915, during World War I. The British ship went down after being torpedoed by a German submarine.*

◀ *The* Queen Mary 2 *liner is repaired in dry dock in Hamburg, Germany.*

rather than driving a piston to and fro. This system converts the energy in the steam into a spinning motion very efficiently, and so turbines were powerful enough to drive huge ships.

These advances in construction and engine design led to the launching of the first great ocean liners. Parsons' turbines powered the great liners of the day, such as the ill-fated *Lusitania,* and later liners got bigger and faster, reaching their high point in the 1920s and 1930s, when giant ships like the *Queen Mary* and *Queen Elizabeth* crossed the Atlantic Ocean in less than a week.

▼ *The largest ships in the world are supertankers, used to transport crude oil. They are at least 1,243 ft (379 m) long—four times the length of a football field.*

FACTS AND FIGURES

● The largest passenger ship ever built is the *Oasis of the Seas* built in 2009. She weighs 225,282 tons (228,897 metric tons) and is 1,187 ft (362 m) long.

● The largest supertanker is the *Mont,* weighing 564,650 tons (555,728 metric tons) deadweight and over 1,500 ft (458 m) long.

● The largest cargo ship is the *Berge Stahl,* weighing 364,767 tons (359,003 metric tons) and 1,125 ft (342 m) long.

● The largest sailing ship was the *France II,* built in 1911 and weighing 5,806 tons (5,714 metric tons). The ship was 418 ft (127 m) long.

Modern developments

Modern oil tankers, like most ships today, are powered by diesel engines, first introduced in 1912, or by gas turbines, first tried in 1947. Attempts with nuclear power, used for the first time in the U.S. government ship *Savannah* of 1962, have so far proved limited. In 1980 the Nippon Kokan shipyard of Japan launched a cargo ship that reduced fuel costs by assisting the engines with large rigid sails, turned to the optimum angle by computer-controlled motors. This idea has yet to be widely adopted.

One of the real limits on the speed a conventional boat can move through the water is the drag of water on its hull, and the most radical changes in boat design in recent years— the hydrofoil, the hovercraft, and the multihull— have been an attempt to solve this problem.

KEY COMPONENTS

Hovercraft

The hovercraft is an amphibious vehicle that rides on a cushion of air over water and land. In 1877 Sir John Thornycroft patented the idea for a hovercraft, but he had a problem—how to prevent the cushion of air escaping from under the craft. It wasn't until the 1950s that this problem was solved by Sir Christopher Cockerell. He added a rubber skirt with inward pointing jets of air.

Hovercraft consist of five main components: the skirt, the lift system, the propulsion system, the hull, and the engine. On large craft the engine is a gas turbine, and this usually powers the propulsion and lift systems. Smaller craft use diesel engines. To create enough lift, high-speed centrifugal fans suck air through intakes on top of the vehicle and force it down through the skirt and under the craft. The skirt is made of nylon and plastic, and is effectively a huge bag that fills with air. The air escapes from the bag through holes facing inward. This creates the air cushion. The bag also provides some support when the vehicle is at rest.

▶ *Hovercraft barely touch the surface as they float on air. That makes it hard to stop them—they will just keep moving until the air cushion runs out.*

Modified aircraft propellers on top of the hovercraft provide propulsion. The propellers pivot for steering and there are rudders at the back. The air cushion makes steering these vehicles difficult. In case of engine failure, hovercraft hulls contain a flotation chamber that stops the craft from sinking.

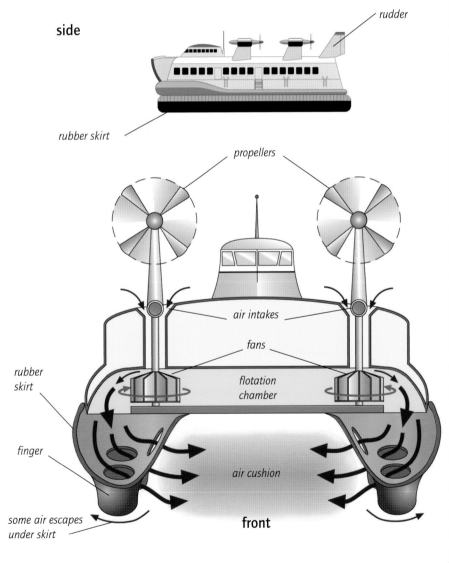

side

rudder

rubber skirt

propellers

air intakes

fans

flotation chamber

rubber skirt

finger

air cushion

some air escapes under skirt

front

▲ *A passenger hydrofoil speeds over the water. Lifting the hull out of the water reduces drag so the vessel can travel at higher speeds that other types of water craft. However, it is not suited to rough weather.*

FACTS AND FIGURES

- The fastest crossing of the Atlantic was Tom Gentry's *Gentry Eagle*, which crossed in just over two-and-a-half days at an average speed of over 45 knots (52 mph, or 83 km/h).
- The water speed record is 300 knots (345 mph, or 556 km/h), held by the hydroplane *Spirit of Australia*.

A hydrofoil is essentially a cross between a waterski and an aircraft wing that projects on legs beneath the hull. When a boat equipped with hydrofoils is moving fast enough, the hydrofoils begin to lift the hull up out of the water. Riding on a cushion of air, hovercraft can travel equally on water and on land. The first hovercraft, built in 1959 by Sir Christopher Cockerel, was only able to carry three passengers at slow speeds and could only travel over calm water or flat ground. Nowadays big hovercraft are used as amphibious landing craft by the military and as commercial ferries, but hovercraft never met expectations. They proved

STICK CHARTS

Ancient sailors did not have satellite navigation or even compasses to show them the way. The islanders of Micronesia made charts of the ocean out of sticks and shells to represent the location of islands and the flow of ocean currents. Some stick charts showed the currents flowing around one island in detail, while others showed how to sail to distant islands.

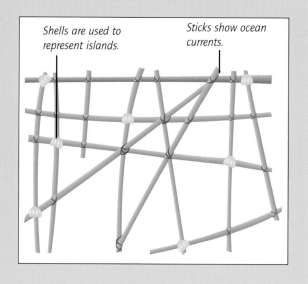

Shells are used to represent islands.

Sticks show ocean currents.

hard to steer, cannot operate well on rough water and can only cross very flat land.

The future

Remarkably, it is with the oldest of all these ideas that the future seems to lie—the multihull. The idea dates back to the earliest boats. The Polynesians built two- or even three-hulled boats. Giving remarkable stability and dipping only narrow hulls into the water, these catamarans (two-hulled boats) could move much faster than conventional boats. Modern sailing catamarans can reach speeds of 37 mph (59 km/h) and there are now multihulled cargo ships and car ferries.

THE FIRST MULTIHULLS?

Most dugout canoes are so heavy and sit so low in the water that they can only be used in calm inland waters. But in the Pacific, by attaching an outrigger (an extra float on the side) or by adding on extra hulls, these log boats became so light and stable that they were once used for great journeys across the ocean. The Pacific islands were probably colonized centuries ago in such multihulled dugouts.

SCIENTIFIC PRINCIPLES

Buoyancy

The ancient Greek philosopher Archimedes realized that an object weighs less in water than air because the upward push, or upthrust, of the water gives it buoyancy. When an object is immersed in water, the object begins to sink under its own weight. But the water pushes it back up with a force equal to the weight of water displaced (pushed out of the way) by the sinking object. The object sinks until its weight is equalled by the upthrust of the water, at which point it floats. Even boats made from iron can float because the air inside the hull makes them weigh less, overall, than water.

Ships display a marking on their sides called the Plimsoll line. This shows the maximum depth to which a ship may be safely loaded under different conditions. A ship's buoyancy depends on its weight but also on the density of the water it sails in. The density of water is affected by its temperature and

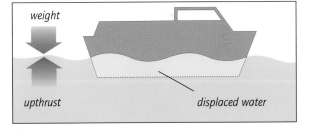

how much salt it contains. Cold salty water is more dense than warm, less saline water. The more dense the water, the more cargo a ship can safely carry. The Plimsoll line was devised in 1875, after British politician Samuel Plimsoll (1824–1898) saw ships carrying dangerous amounts of cargo. All ships have used one since 1939.

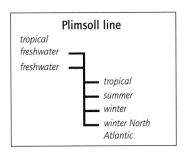

Plimsoll line
tropical
freshwater
freshwater

tropical
summer
winter
winter North
Atlantic

3500 B.C. Wheels are added to sleds to make the first carts.

3000 B.C. Horses are domesticated in Central Asia and used for riding.

2500 B.C. Skis invented in Scandinavia made from wood and animal fur.

1900 B.C. The Mesopotamians develop the spoked wheel.

1300 B.C. The Hyksos invent the horse bit, a piece of metal placed between the horse's teeth that gives the rider more control.

250 B.C. Eratosthenes draws a map of the world that includes lines of longitude and latitude.

A.D. 100 Stirrups are invented to help riders stay seated at full gallop.

600s The modern design of saddle is introduced by the Scythians of eastern Europe.

1100s The first true sailing warship, the cog, is built in Europe.

1400 A horse-drawn carriage with a suspension system is invented in Kocs, Hungary, becoming known as the coach.

1490 A bicycle with two wheels, pedals, and a chain drive to the back wheel is designed by Leonardo da Vinci.

1493 Christopher Columbus crosses the Atlantic in a caravel, a sailing ship employing square and lanteen (triangular) sails to enhance maneuverability.

1550 Railroads are invented in Europe for use in mines.

1712 Thomas Newcomen develops a steam engine for removing water from mines.

1769 Nicholas Joseph Cugnot builds the first self-propelled road vehicle, an enormous steam carriage. It is involved in the first road traffic accident when it runs out of control.

1775 John Outram invents the streetcar, also known as the "tram" in many countries.

1782 James Watts invents the double-acting steam engine, an improvement on his engines that produce rotary motion.

1801 Richard Trevithick builds a steam-powered carriage.

1812 The first practical steam railroad starts operating between Leeds and Middleton in England.

1819 Karl von Drais introduces the Laumaschine, or Running Machine, the first design of bicycle.

1829 George Stephenson unveils his steam-powered locomotive, *Rocket*, designed mainly by his son Robert.

1830 The first American railroad opens in Charleston, South Carolina.

1839 Charles Goodyear finds that rubber can be made more stable by heating with sulfur, a process later named vulcanization.

1849 The block signaling system for railroads is invented. An automatic version using electricity is introduced in 1867.

1860s Pierre Lallement constructs the first bicycle with pedals. The machine is called a velocipede.

1863 First underground railroad, or subway, opens in London.

1867 Nikolaus August Otto makes the first working internal-combustion engine that uses the four-stroke cycle.

1868 The first bicycle race is held in Paris.

1885 Gottlieb Daimler builds the first modern motorcycle. Karl Benz builds a three-wheeled car in the same year

1888 The pneumatic tire is invented by John Boyd Dunlop.

1908 Henry Ford starts mass producing the Model T, bringing automobiles within the reach of ordinary people.

1912 The first diesel locomotive is built.

1979 The *Seawise Giant* supertanker, later renamed *Mont*, is launched in Japan. It is the largest vehicle every built.

2003 A maglev train becomes the fastest vehicle to travel on a railroad.

2009 The *Oasis of the Seas*, the largest passenger ship ever built, is launched.

2011 Bloodhound is the first car built to travel faster than 1,000 mph (1,600 km/h).

GLOSSARY

airfoil A curved surface that is designed to create a lift force when a fluid—such as air or water—flows around it. Wings are airfoils, and the blades of a ship's propeller have a similar shape.

ancient Greece A civilization that existed on the mainland and islands of modern-day Greece and Turkey between 2000 and 300 B.C.

beast of a burden A domesticated animal that is used to carry heavy loads (burdens) or pull a cart.

benzene A highly poisonous liquid derived from petroleum, or crude oil, and used for making plastics and other medicines. Benzene was also the fuel used in the first internal-combustion engines.

buoyancy Whether an object will sink or float in a liquid.

bulkhead A wall that runs across a ship, dividing up the hull.

calliper A hinged device that can open and close in a pinch. Callipers are used in the brakes of most bicycles.

catalytic converter A device that turns many of the poisonous and dangerous gases in exhaust into safer substances. A "cat" works by pulling exhaust gases through a mesh made from special metals, which force the substances to transform into safer chemicals before they are released into the air.

centrifugal Relating to a force that seems to pull a thing outward as it rotates around an axis.

density A measure of how much material is packed into a substance.

diesel A liquid fuel that is heavier and thicker than gasoline. It burns at a higher temperature and is used to power larger engines and vehicles, such as trucks, trains and ships.

domesticated Animals or plants that have been adapted by selective breeding over many generations to live in close association with humans and perform some useful function are described as domesticated.

drag A force that opposes the motion of an object through a fluid such as air or water. Also known as air or water resistance.

electromagnet An iron core surrounded by a coil of copper wire that temporarily generates a magnetic field when an electric current flows through the wire. An electromagnet is useful because its magnetic field can be turned on and off when necessary.

exhaust The gases produced when a fuel burns. When gasoline burns most of the exhaust is carbon dioxide and water. The energy in this hot gas is harnessed to create motion in the engine, before it is pushed out of the engine, and vehicle, via a tailpipe, funnel, or smokestack.

friction The force created when objects rub against each other. Friction is the force that forms a tire's grip. Low-friction surfaces, such as ice, are very slippery.

gravity A natural force that attracts two masses toward one another. The larger object pulls harder than the smaller one Among its many effects, gravity draws objects toward Earth's surface and keeps the planets in orbit around the Sun.

Hittites A people that lived in central Turkey about 4,000 years ago. The Hittites are credited with developing many technologies, including the use of iron.

hydraulic Operated by the movement and force of a liquid. Most hydraulic systems consist of a series of liquid-filled tubes through which a force can be transmitted.

Industrial Revolution A great change in social and economic organization brought about by the replacement of hand tools by machines and power tools, and the development of large-scale industrial production methods. The Industrial Revolution started in England around 1760 and spread to the rest of Europe and the United States.

inertia The universal property of any object which makes it stay in its current state of motion—still or on the move—until a force acts to change it.

internal-combustion engine An engine that uses the hot gases formed when the fuel burns, or combusts, to create motion in the pistons or other moving parts. A gasoline engine does this, while a steam engine is an external-combustion design. The heat from the fuel is used to turn a second substance—water—into a gas, which is then used to create motion.

levitation To float in the air when an upward force is balancing out gravity.

magnetism All phenomena associated with magnets and magnetic fields. Magnetic fields are regions around magnets in which a force acts on any magnet or electric charge present.

magnets Any material capable of generating a magnetic field. *See also* magnetism.

mass The measure of material in an object.

Mesopotamia The name for the land around the Euphrates and Tigris rivers which flow from Turkey and Syria through Iraq to the Persian Gulf. This name means "between the rivers," and the region was one the first places to have cities and civilizations.

Nazi The name of a political party or its members that, led by Adolf Hitler, ruled Germany from 1933 to 1945. The Nazis suppressed all opposition and built up Germany's military strength. They were the main protagonists of World War II.

nomads People who, instead of having a fixed home, travel from place to place in search of fresh pastures and water for themselves and their animals.

omnibus The old-fashioned name for bus. The *omni-* part of the word means "all" in Latin and so an omnibus was a public vehicle that could be used by anyone.

pantograph The conductor on the roof of an electric railroad locomotive or streetcar. The pantograph is lowered when unused, but raised to make contact with power cables running above the track, supplying the train with power.

pivot A turning point.

Roman The ancient civilization that began in the Italian city of Rome around 700 B.C. and had established a vast empire around the Mediterranean Sea by 200 A.D.

Scandinavia A region of northern Europe, usually consisting of Norway, Sweden and Denmark. This region's history includes the famous Norse people, or Vikings.

temperature A measure of how much energy is contained within an object.

transmission An assembly of parts in a motor vehicle, including gear wheels and shafts, that transmits power from the engine to the axles and wheels.

torque The turning effect of a force, when an straight-line, up-and-down force is converted into a rotational force, such as when an engine spins wheels. A small force can produce a large torque if it is applied from a long distance, using a long lever. A force applied closer to the pivot creates a smaller torque.

turbine A machine made up of a set of blades mounted on a central shaft. A moving fluid, such as steam or air, makes the assembly rotate. Turbines are often used to drive generators.

turnpike A barrier or gate that crosses a road where a toll charge was made before road users could continue on their way. Today, turnpike is also used to mean any highway where a toll is charged.

FURTHER RESOURCES

Books

Hear That Train Whistle Blow!: How the Railroad Changed the World by Milton Meltzer. New York: Random House, 2004.

The Legendary Model T Ford: The Ultimate History of America's First Great Automobile by Tom Collins. Iola, WI: Krause Publications, 2007.

Our Transportation Systems by Dorothy Francis. Brookfield, CN: Millbrook Press, 2002.

Ships and Submarines by Chris Woodford. New York: Facts On File, Inc., 2004.

The Transcontinental Railroad and The Great Race to Connect the Nation by Wim Coleman & Pat Perrin. Berkeley Heights, NJ: MyReportLinks.com Books, 2006.

Websites

Library of Congress History of U.S. Railroads with Maps
http://memory.loc.gov/ammem/gmdhtml/rrhtml/rrintro.html

Discovery Channel: History of Cars Timeline
http://www.yourdiscovery.com/cars/timeline/

Royal Navy Ships from 1420 to Today
http://www.royalnavy.mod.uk/history/ships/index.htm

History Timeline of the Bicycle
http://www.pedalinghistory.com/phhistory.html

INDEX